PER
LOVE CASTS
OUT ALL FEAR

Preparing the Bride of Christ
For Jesus' Return

1/7/2018

Dan + Debbie,

I pray the Lord's bountiful blessings over you + Debbie. God bless you guys!

Victor Torres

Victor Torres

VICTOR TORRES

CONTENTS

DEDICATION

This book is dedicated to my Lord and Savior, Jesus Christ, who inspired me to begin writing this manuscript in 1991, and to the many hurting people who have been plagued by tormenting fear. After having seen so many people suffer, I was prompted by the Holy Spirit to write a book that would dare to examine the origins of fear, the negative coping mechanisms that people hide behind and a plan of action to help them overcome their trepidation. I grew to a point where I was deeply troubled by so many victims who agonize daily over heartache, tragedy and despair because they lack the necessary tools or resources in how to combat these monsters.

We will all experience loss in our lives at one point or another. Whether our loss involves the death of a spouse or child, divorce, foreclosure of a home, unemployment or rejection from a failed relationship, the emotional pain is still the same. Our hearts still ache, our dreams are shattered and our memories are forever scarred. Alfred Lord Tennyson in a poem he wrote in 1850 said, "…'Tis better to have loved and lost than never to have loved at all." Love is worth experiencing and fighting for, despite the pain that comes later.

With this in mind, I pray that this manuscript will help many people to weather the storms of life that they are forced to face. I trust that as you read through the pages of this labor of love that you will listen with an open heart and mind and become equipped in battling and defeating fear and inner demons that have no right to torment you. I trust that the Savior of this world will become more real to you than ever before as you gain understanding and truly realize that perfect love (which comes from God) casts out all fear.

I know you will find many answers here that your heart has longed to discover. I'm here to announce that your wait is over!

You are not destined to suffer emotionally all of your life. Fight on, my friends and valiant warriors, because emotional healing belongs to you. Take it and receive it! I am cheering you on because the best years of your life are ahead of you. I am deeply honored that you are seeking answers here and I trust that you won't be disappointed as you learn about and take to heart spiritual truths that will bring you emotional freedom and spiritual direction.

ACKNOWLEDGEMENTS

I acknowledge my mother and father, Calixto and Josefina Torres, who were both Christian-Catholics and are in Heaven now. You raised me with high moral values and challenged me to fulfill my potential. I am deeply indebted to you for giving me a straight and narrow path that provided me with clear direction at a young age.

I give special thanks to my best friend, Neal Kanzler, who has encouraged me the last 22 years in my Christian faith, including fulfilling my dream to become a published author. Neal, you have been there for me during some of the happiest and darkest times of my life. I am deeply indebted to you for your prayers, emotional support, wisdom and friendship.

I thank Rayford Johnson, my good friend, author of Thug Mentality Exposed, motivational speaker, and photojournalist, who has provided me with much affirmation and direction in becoming a published author and inspirational speaker. I highly value your wisdom, guidance and encouragement. I would also like to thank Erik Sanders, my graphic artist, for doing a superb job with the front and back covers and internal lay-out of my book. You did a phenomenal job, Erik, and I am deeply honored to have worked with you on this project and I appreciate all the hard work you put into helping me see my manuscript become a published work of art with your creative, finishing touches.

I give thanks to my mentors and good friends, Pastor Joseph and Irene Yong, Pastor Eddie Green, David Reyes, and my text reader, Debbie Phillips, who helped me to make sure my manuscript was biblically sound, relevant and edifying to hurting individuals. I am very grateful to all of you for investing your time in my book and I pray God's blessings over you.

I would also like to thank Alison Neumann, a precious friend who I've had the pleasure of getting to know this year. You are the sweetest, most loving and kindest woman I have ever met. I have never met anyone with such a pure, humble heart who desires to do what is right so you can please the Lord. I commend you highly for your work with children who have special needs and I greatly admire your skills and expertise. Your calling pleases the very heart of God. I am very proud of you for how you have overcome great storms in your life with God's help. The Lord has used you as a tremendous inspiration in my life in many ways and especially in helping me to finish writing this book through the model of what a beautiful, virtuous, Christian woman is all about. Thank you, Ali, for being my special friend. I am very honored and deeply humbled to know you!

Finally, I would like to thank my son, Joshua Torres, a very gifted writer, scholar, and editor for editing my book. You are very meticulous in your work and I greatly appreciate all the time and effort that you painstakingly put into the editing process. You truly have a very bright future. I am very proud of you!

INTRODUCTION

Fear is a killer in our society. It claims the young and old, the educated and uneducated, the rich and the poor, and religious and non-religious people. It is no respecter of persons. Its aim is to maim, kill, and destroy. It shows no mercy for its millions of victims. Fear is like a hurricane that can't be stopped, a towering inferno that can't be quenched, and a deadly plague that kills at such an alarming rate that we are often left helpless, hopeless and crying for mercy.

Fear manifests itself through worry, anxiety, stress and even death. It literally forces children and adults to go into hiding. We hide behind coping mechanisms such as invisible masks, mind-games and imaginary walls that temporarily shield us from imminent danger. We stuff our emotional hurts behind these protective shields to minimize our excruciating pain and nagging discomfort. Unfortunately, no one tells us that these powerful mind-games gradually steal our health, wealth and emotional freedom.

For many of us, the best we can do is merely survive, so we make a pact with such evils as denial, blaming, catastrophizing and perfectionism to help us weather these horrifying storms. Often, not knowing any better, we fail to realize that this is like making a pact with the Devil because this evil presence always requires payment later. What follows is a very rich, in-depth look at the many negative coping mechanisms that we rely on and the harmful, deadly effects they have on us, our loved ones and our relationship with God.

We will take a genuine look at the true condition of your heart, your thought life and your healthy and unhealthy patterns to help you move out of your desert wasteland and into the Promised Land, the land that so many people seek, but seldom find. It is your divine destiny to dwell in such a paradise here on this earth and find rest as you discover what it means to live in God's perfect love. You will find that perfect love casts out all fear and once you learn how powerful love is you'll realize that

you'll never have any reason to dwell in a prison of fear again.

Finally, we'll explore what it means to live an abundant life where you thrive with happiness, peace, and joy and not just survive as a pauper anymore. You'll discover that the only one who can stop you from reaching your destination is you and as you learn to exercise courage, you'll secure your reservations with the Promised Land that awaits you. You have a rendezvous with your divine destiny and it is waiting for you here within the pages of your life that follow.

It is your mission to slay fear and to embrace courage and pure love. Then, after you have defeated your Goliaths, you will do as King David did when he danced unashamedly with all his might. I commission you now to go after your emotional freedom, my friend, and do not allow anyone or anything to stop you. Enjoy the journey!

CHAPTER ONE

DWELLING IN FEAR

**"There is a way that seems right to a man,
but its end is the way of death."
(Proverbs 14:12)**

We live in a world of fear. Every day we see acts of violence in the media. We hear of horrible crimes being committed by children, barely in their teens. We buy alarms, locks and security systems to protect our homes and cars. And as for our personal lives, many of us have learned how to live on a superficial level to keep others at a distance because we don't want to give anyone an opportunity to hurt us. We build up "walls," therefore, to insulate us from heartache, and we choose to do anything but be entirely truthful, not only with those around us, but also with God and ourselves.

We use these behaviors to try to gain control when our world seems out of control. Instead, they force us into a superficial means of survival. Just like a tumbleweed growing in the desert, we appear to be healthy and green on the outside but when the winds of calamity blow, we are torn up and tossed to and fro without mercy on the inside because we have no deep root of faith in Jesus.

Our insecurities cause us to put up a false image, an imitation of who we really are because we're afraid that we'll be ridiculed, laughed at, or abused for being real. So, we lock ourselves in our "ivory towers" and retreat emotionally from the people we blame for causing us pain. Content now that no one can penetrate our defenses, we quite often don't realize that neither can we get out. Unfortunately, we have also unknowingly locked out the only One who holds the key: Jesus!

As children, we hide behind imaginary walls. We do this naturally, especially when someone tramples on our feelings. We also seek refuge under our blankets when we go to bed because we're afraid of monsters that lurk in the night. Bullies were monsters to me and I still have vivid memories as a child when a mean-spirited thug belittled me through his racist comments.

He told me, "You're nothing but a dumb, worthless Mexican; you'll never go anywhere in life. Go back to Mexico where you came from, you stupid spic!" The worst part about this experience was not the filth that spewed out of this young man's vile mouth, but the simple fact that he publicly shamed me in front of my friends.

I felt so angry that I wanted to deal with this bully the way vigilante Paul Kersey, who starred as Charles Bronson, so promptly disposed of one of the hard-core criminals who murdered his wife and raped his daughter in the movie, *Death Wish*. After he cornered Stomper, the criminal, Mr. Kersey turned to him and asked, "Do you believe in Jesus?" Thinking that he might show him some mercy, he replied with a frantic, "Yes, I do!" Paul coldly responded with, "Well, you're gonna meet Him!" [1] And then, he blew the criminal away!

Of course, in real life I would never take the law into my own hands, especially because Romans 12:20 warns us that we should not repay evil with evil because vengeance belongs to the Lord. I was raised with and practiced religious values and I loved my parents too much to cause them unnecessary pain and heartache by going down a destructive path. However, the fantasy world provided me with a place that I could safely escape to where I could channel my deep hurts and anger. Or so, I thought.

In reality, I felt very ashamed and deeply rejected, but mostly humiliated when my heart was bloodied by these social deviants for their good pleasure. I was clueless as far as what to do. So, I quietly stuffed one offensive remark after another into the deep recesses of my wounded spirit to help numb my pain.

Though I experienced some temporary relief, I had no idea that my hidden sorrow would eventually transform itself into hideous monsters that I had never met before. They were called "bitterness," "unforgiveness," and "unresolved anger." I became a walking time-bomb, though I did not fully comprehend this concept back then. Not only was I victimized by bullies, but even worse, I victimized myself out of ignorance by putting my trust in negative coping mechanisms.

RECOGNIZING THE MANY FACES OF FEAR

In order to acquire a full understanding of where these unhealthy behavior patterns come from, we need to examine "the original sin." In Genesis 2:16-17 the Lord said "Of every tree of the garden you may freely eat; but of the tree of the knowledge of good and evil you shall not eat, for in the day that you eat of it you shall surely die." God's command to Adam was clear in order that he could remain protected from evil and so that he would not taste death.

However, in the third chapter of Genesis we find that Satan convinced Eve to disobey the Lord by instilling in her the fear that God had lied to her and her husband and that He was withholding the fruit from them unfairly. Both Adam and Eve succumbed to this fear and rationalized that they had "every right" to break God's command to not eat of the tree and thus overstepped the boundaries that God had laid out for them.

By choosing to rebel against the Lord and taste the only fruit in the Garden that was forbidden, they produced "fruit" of their own: when God confronted the man, Adam was in denial and attempted to avoid his problem by hiding from Him. Adam lied, minimized, made excuses and blamed the woman when the Lord asked him if he ate from the tree. When God confronted the woman she also reacted in the same fashion, except she blamed the serpent instead. The woman allowed herself to be deceived, lied to and manipulated by Satan, as did the man by the woman. Both failed to assume responsibility for their transgressions.

Comedian Flip Wilson used to dress up and act like a woman in his nightclub acts in the 1960s and 70s and declare, "The devil made me do it!" He was very entertaining with his mannerisms and facial expressions and quite convincing as he drew considerable laughter for his remarkable humor. [2] What made Wilson's line so funny were his antics and the popular notion that it was acceptable to blame someone else for our shortcomings.

And yet, as funny as this comedian was in using the enemy of our souls as a scapegoat, rest assured that God will hold us responsible for every transgression that we commit. We are solely responsible for the sins of our flesh and the sooner we own up to our corruption and reconcile with God, the more assurance we'll have that our eternity in Heaven is secure. If we are truly Christians, we must choose to live pure lives for the Lord on a daily basis.

As a result of allowing Satan to plant fear in their hearts, Adam and Eve sinned by defying God's boundaries for their lives. And, because they transgressed against His commands, they received the judgment of eventual death. This happened not just physically, but in every aspect of their beings: spiritually, they were separated from the Lord, and emotionally, mentally and relationally, they were separated from each other by the very behaviors they had used in their vain attempt to cover up their sin.

Then, instead of responding with humility and repentant hearts, they panicked and hid themselves when they heard their Heavenly Father coming toward them in the Garden. Adam and Eve were dealt a severe blow when they allowed Satan to influence and deceive them. This is how the enemy keeps us in bondage today: he manipulates us into rejecting the truth and believing a lie, thus allowing fear to drive a wedge between us and God.

BELIEVING LIES LEADS TO OUR IMPRISONMENT

Sometime in adulthood, we'll realize that the unhealthy behaviors which once helped us to avoid emotional suffering no longer work. Yes, that means there was a time when these types of survival mechanisms served a valuable purpose. Perhaps they aided us in warding off suicidal thoughts, helped us to cope with the divorce or death of our parents, or assisted us in surviving an incident of rape or molestation.

They shielded us at a time when we didn't know what else to do until we established a personal relationship with Jesus Christ and allowed Him to save us from our sins, heal our damaged emotions and deliver us from destructive lifestyles. After we matured in the Lord, however, we should have been able to discern (if we haven't already) that these survival mechanisms were merely mind-games. They no longer are effective in shielding us from real hurt, for this simple reason: the pain which is tormenting us is not on the outside; it's on the inside!

Unfortunately, many of us have allowed Satan to fool us into thinking, "Well, maybe life is supposed to be this way." Satan is a liar and the father of all lies (John 8:44). He desires to keep you shackled as a prisoner of your misperceptions for the rest of your life.

If you belong to Christ, Satan doesn't own the property rights to you anymore, but he'll do everything in his power to influence you to doubt God's Word and to make you think the Lord doesn't care about you. If he can defeat you with his lies, then you won't live as if the Bible is true and you won't trust God to heal you of your wounds. And you certainly won't stand firm in the power and authority that you have in Jesus to tell the enemy of your soul to get lost!

Jesus proclaimed in Luke 4:18-19, "The Spirit of the Lord is upon Me, because He has anointed Me to preach the gospel to the poor; He has sent Me to heal the brokenhearted, to proclaim liberty to the captives and recovery of sight to the blind, to set at liberty those who are oppressed; to proclaim the acceptable year of the Lord" [emphasis author's]. However, walking in Jesus' footsteps requires embracing the very qualities that we have learned to shun: openness, honesty and vulnerability. Yes, we can go on existing in our self-created prison of fear, but in the end, the only one laughing at us will be Satan. He knows that if we allow anxiety to consume us, our witness will be ineffective and we'll be rendered useless for the kingdom of God.

Have you constructed a mighty fortress of lies which needs to be demolished? Are its walls buttressed with fear? Jesus will dismantle that deceptive infrastructure once you allow Him to. You'll discover He is easier on you than you are on yourself because He doesn't tear down His people; He just tears down destructive walls that have been constructed by fearful individuals.

He won't use your rugged sledgehammer the way you've used it whenever you've made a mistake, continually beating yourself. He uses a smoother, finer instrument. Metaphorically speaking, Jesus uses His finely-made chisel, the Holy Spirit, to perform His loving, delicate work—to break off the sharp ends, remove the glaring defects, smooth out the rough edges and carefully shape us to look more like Him and less like our old selves. After the Lord has refined us through the kiln or a fiery trial, we will no longer see any traces of fear (until the next test) because God perfects us through His love.

At the same time, God will establish a foundation for us built on faith, and faith alone, so that no evil influence known to mankind can ever destroy it. Psalm 127:1 declares that: "unless the Lord builds the house, they labor in vain who build it..." Jesus is the Master Craftsman, and even though He must tear down the ugly things that we have erected, He will build us up again as "living stones" to be "a spiritual house, a holy priesthood, to offer up spiritual sacrifices acceptable to God through Jesus Christ" (1 Peter 2:5).

FACING OUR HURTS

What keeps you from disclosing the deep wounds or offenses in your life? Is it shame? Guilt? Fear? False Pride? Who told you to keep a secret or you would suffer harm? How long will you allow this wound to haunt you? If you have a hurt and pretend the pain doesn't exist, it is sin. Why? Because you are not being honest and you are living a lie! You are continuing to consume the same forbidden fruit that the Lord commanded Adam and Eve not to eat—the fruit of disobedience, rebellion and lack of trust in God.

Once you ingest it, it poisons your heart and mind and teaches you to become more cunning at lying, criticizing, manipulating and cheating. In other words, sin begets sin. Why would you want to become more like Satan? Why would you desire to become craftier at deceiving yourself and others by pretending that your turmoil does not exist?

We are reminded in 1 John 1:9-10 that "If we confess our sins, He is faithful and just to forgive us our sins and to cleanse us from all unrighteousness. If we say that we have not sinned, we make Him a liar, and His Word is not in us." Therefore, if we hide dark secrets, concealed sins or hurts in our lives that we've carried for years, we're really saying we don't trust that God is powerful or wise enough to heal us and we are calling Him a liar!

Jesus is the Master Surgeon; He will take the old festering wounds embedded deep in our hearts and gently clean out the infections of hatred, anger, unforgiveness, bitterness, shame and guilt. One of the most beautiful promises to me in the Bible is Jeremiah 30:17, "For I will restore health to you and heal you of your wounds…" What awesome love! What wonderful grace! He will heal us! He will restore "the years that the… locust has eaten" (Joel 2:25)!

However, that means that you'll need to lay still on the operating table long enough for the Great Physician to finish His work in you (Mark 2:17).

That means that you'll need to trust the Good Shepherd even when He leads you "through the valley of the shadow of death" (Psalm 23:4).

That means that you'll need to give the Vinedresser permission to cut away the old, dead wood so you can flourish and bear much fruit (John 15:1-2).

That means that you'll need to endure labor pains (John 16:21-24) before you can rejoice in what God is birthing in you: a pure, spotless Bride, wholly set apart for Himself.

Honestly dealing with our emotional pain rather than stuffing our hurts reminds me of a conversation I had with a friend, Cliff Lane, many years ago. As we were conversing, God gave us a picture of what it's like when we put off facing our afflictions. Have you ever seen driftwood floating on top of the ocean? What happens when you push it down under the water and then let it go? It not only comes up, but it comes up violently! So, you must exercise caution and move out of the way quickly so it doesn't seriously injure you when it surfaces from its suppressed state. Trust me, that wood does not care whether you've been baptized or not—If you mess with it, it will leave a memorable imprint on your forehead!

Through this image, God shows us that our emotions are not any different. When we stuff our pain for an extended period of time, a day will come when our wounds will demand payment and release from prison. The result is often a violent outburst in very much the same way in which a balloon explodes, a volcano erupts, or an out-of-control airplane smashes into a mountain.

Our feelings have a date with a crash landing when they've been neglected and not managed properly. That's because they've been forced to exist on borrowed time while they've been falsely accused and innocently chained in a dungeon. A day will come when our repressed emotions will demand justice and maybe even revenge.

For these reasons, you don't mess with driftwood for the same reason that you don't mess with a rattlesnake—it can strike you with ferocity and poison you from within. If that happens, you may wind up in urgent care. It's much easier, wiser, and healthier to manage your troubles when they come up. Otherwise, you may be dealing with something more serious like depression, suicide, or even murder (Genesis 4:6-11). Don't go there!

Learn how to manage your emotions before they manage you. Leave behind your life of survival by being honest from within so you can experience emotional and spiritual revival instead! Psalm 51:6 clearly states, "Behold, You desire truth in the inward parts, and in the hidden part You will make me to know wisdom." A wise man or woman chooses to live a life of integrity that is pleasing to God.

HOW, THEN, SHOULD WE LIVE?

As Christian people, we are called to take off the graveclothes we once wore. Denial, rationalizing and manipulating should be a part of our past, not our present or our future! These deadly, poisonous fruits have only served to postpone (and thus, intensify) our difficulties until a later time in our lives. When we eat of them, we swallow the lie from our enemy that we need not face our pain now, but we can wait until later when it's more convenient. Satan does not tell us, however, that our hurt will be magnified many times over when we opt to face it in the future instead.

It's like using a credit card. When we fail to pay it off month in and month out, the debt accumulates. Then, when we finally realize it, we find that our spending has grown out of control because we hadn't realized how much we were going to be charged for interest. Hundreds eventually become thousands of dollars owed. Satan will never tell us the truth when it comes to being honest about facing our distraught emotions (or about anything, for that matter).

We must not listen to the voice that whispers: "Wait

until tomorrow to face this pain. You have more important matters to take care of right now." If we continue to listen to such deception, we'll find ourselves back in the same graveyard that Christ pulled us from when He first saved us and came to dwell in our hearts (Ephesians 2:1).

Your days of surviving like a mummy or an emotional stiff are over! Your Heavenly Father has a specific plan of restoration for every hurt that you'll ever face. Let Jesus take off those old bandages, just like He did when He raised Lazarus from the dead. Your former ways of wandering in the graveyard must be left in the past. So, take off those fearful, burial clothes and decide it's time to live again in your rightful, resurrected state.

IS THE INSIDE AS CLEAN AS THE OUTSIDE?

Many people are content to simply put on embellished facades and Sunday morning smiles so others will think everything is fine in their lives. They're unwilling to do the deep cleansing work needed to mature in their faith. A wall of pride has clouded their vision and convinced them it's more convenient to live as a fake for appearances' sake. Little do they realize that they've given Satan free access and are, therefore, being used as his puppet through a spirit of deception that they've chosen to survive by.

Think for a moment: how many people do you know of who have left church because of "the hypocrites?" Merely attending church services and waiting to hear from God through a preacher only on Sundays is not the same as having a zealous desire for holiness that's firmly established through an active prayer and devotional life. Often, a discerning person will be able to see right through your phoniness because the walls to your heart have holes in them that are constructed with lies and reek with deceit under the heat of God's hand that separates the wheat from the chaff with unquenchable fire (Matthew 3:12).

The wheat represents those who are truly repentant— those who have sincere hearts and desire to follow Christ with reverent adoration. Chaff, on the other hand, is the husk that surrounds a seed that is typically thrown away; waste material. [3]

When I visualize chaff, I see fearful individuals who construct coping mechanisms or imaginary walls of fear that temporarily shield them from emotional pain that will come back to haunt them later.

This reminds me of the Pharisees and Sadducees who always looked good on the outside, but were unrepentant and satisfied with their feeble, spiritual condition on the inside. A true Christian must always allow the unquenchable fire, the Holy Spirit, to burn away all negative defense mechanisms that would tempt him to gradually fall away from God.

God makes it clear that He does not judge our character by outward appearances, but by the heart (1 Samuel 16:7). He also declares in Isaiah 29:13 that He will judge those who "... draw near with their mouths and honor Me with their lips, but have removed their hearts far from Me..." As the Lord's new creations, we should only be associated with God's truth and living a pure life.

If old things have truly passed away, and all things have indeed become new since our conversion to Christ, then that should include how we conduct ourselves. If it doesn't, then why even call ourselves Christians, since we live a lie? If Jesus Christ is truly our Lord and Savior, then we should trust Him to lead our hearts in how to live an abundant life. Let's not forget the freedom that 2 Corinthians 5:17 reveals, "Therefore, if anyone is in Christ, he is a new creation; old things have passed away; behold, all things have become new."

ABUNDANT LIVING IN CHRIST

How does God heal our deep wounds? He gives us new hearts! In Ezekiel 11:14-25 the Lord talks about the process involved in restoration. He proclaims in verses 19-20:

> Then I will give them one heart, and I will put
> a new spirit within them, and take the stony
> heart out of their flesh, and give them a heart
> of flesh, that they may walk in My statutes and
> keep My judgments and do them, and they
> shall be My people, and I will be their God.

God gave His people a heart of flesh for a purpose—so our hearts could be pliable, moldable, and stretchable so we could be rid of our unhealthy ways of existing in order that we can serve the Lord with a complete heart, and thus live an abundant life. Proverbs 4:23 says "Keep your heart with all diligence, for out of it spring the issues of life."

Have you ever met someone with a heart of stone? This kind of individual is unable to show genuine compassion towards other people because he's chosen to become so hardened that he doesn't feel sorrow when distressing experiences come his way. Why? Because he has interpreted moments of affliction from his past as being so negative that he doesn't want anything to do with such hurtful memories ever again. This individual has conditioned himself to become numb to all types of grief-stricken ordeals. To him, feelings equal pain.

Tom was a Vietnam War veteran who had been specially trained as a Green Beret. Toward the end of a class on reconciliation that we took together, Pastor Paul Goulet, our instructor, was led by the Holy Spirit to pray specifically for people plagued by overwhelming heartache. After watching other followers of Christ weep freely and receive God's healing touch, Tom desired to receive the same gift.

He described how he had taken part in a great deal of death and destruction of innocent men, women and children. Because he had shut down his emotions as a means of survival, he had become so hardened to tragic events that he hadn't cried in over twenty years. As Pastor Paul prayed for Tom, another veteran prayed over him, too.

Shortly after, the Holy Spirit restored Tom's ability to shed tears by breaking down the powerful denial system that had made him a prisoner of war for two excruciating decades—long after this brutal conflict had ended. In just a few moments, God took this man from a life of survival to a state of revival; one that embraced abundant living in Christ. A heart of stone became a heart of flesh as Tom trusted the Lord to give him a brand new life. God was faithful that night to hear his cry for freedom and to grant his heart's request.

I don't believe Tom knew when he chose to not face the truth as he did, that he would remain in that superficial state for such a lengthy time or that he'd be unable to break free from that stronghold on his own. He attempted to cry for many years since the Vietnam War ended, but was unable to do so. As a result, he was haunted by severe depression.

This gives us an idea of how powerful mind-games can be and how the enemy uses them against us in an attempt to strangle and eventually kill us. Any time we shut down our emotions we're at risk of becoming severely stressed and depressed. This can lead to more serious issues such as alcoholism, drug abuse or even suicide.

Jesus broke the stronghold in Tom's life and he's a walking miracle today! If you've ever experienced such a miracle, you know that prior to this marvelous event taking place that you had to make a conscious choice to face your dilemma. You likely came to a point where you realized there was no other means by which you were going to receive God's healing touch until you finally told the Lord, "Okay, Jesus. I'm willing. Go ahead and do whatever you have to do." This required honesty, courage and faith on your part, but you did it. With this in mind, history is on your side. If you trusted Jesus before, you can trust Him again.

Or perhaps you've been deceived by Satan into believing that either God can't heal you or doesn't love you enough to heal you. These are both lies! If you've never experienced His healing touch in the area of your emotions, be encouraged in knowing that the Lord is more than able to perform such a miracle work in your life. Each time He answers a prayer request, let it strengthen your resolve to trust Him and write it down so you can keep a record of His faithfulness. Believe that the Lord will continue to answer your petitions because He loves you.

Are you ready to receive the tender heart that He desires to give you? If you choose to place your heart of stone in Christ's hands, He promises in His Word (Ezekiel 11:19-20) to give you a new, loving one. Just believe the Word and receive your healing.

BELIEVING AND RECEIVING
THE PROMISE

The Bible talks about living an abundant life in Christ. The word "abundance" means "an extremely plentiful or over-sufficient quantity or supply; more than adequate or having great quantity; richly supplied; overflowing fullness: abundance of the heart." [4] In John 10:10, Jesus proclaims, "The thief does not come except to steal, and to kill, and to destroy. I have come that they may have life, and that they may have it more abundantly."

Satan's primary goal is to destroy the believer. One ploy that he's used repeatedly on us, especially when we're experiencing emotional turmoil, is to influence us to believe that all we have to do to overcome stormy weather is to trust in the fear-filled survival skills we learned early on. He wants us to believe that rationalizing, denial, stuffing our feelings, or putting on a mask will suffice in protecting us from painful intruders, and that trusting the Living God who teaches us new ways of living is not necessary.

Psalm 36:7-8 says that those who trust in the Lord's protection will be "abundantly satisfied with the fullness of Your [God's] house, and You give them drink from the river of Your pleasures." The apostle Paul also addresses the abundant life in Christ in Ephesians 3:14-21. He boldly declares:

> For this reason I bow my knees to the Father of our Lord Jesus Christ... that He would grant you, according to the riches of His glory, to be strengthened with might through His Spirit in the inner man, that Christ may dwell in your hearts through faith; that you, being rooted and grounded in love [not fear], may be able to comprehend... what is the width and length and depth and height—to know the love of Christ which passes knowledge; that you may be filled with all the fullness of God.

> Now to Him who is able to do exceedingly
> <u>abundantly</u> above all that we ask or think,
> according to the power that works in us, to
> Him be glory in the church by Christ Jesus
> through all generations forever and ever.
> Amen. [Emphasis author's]

Paul makes it clear in these passages that it is Jesus who strengthens us, dwells in our hearts, and heals us through His love. Our old way of surviving (which was influenced by our flesh and Satan) should no longer have any root in us because we are now rooted and grounded in Christ (Ephesians 3:14-19) and He represents love and newness of life .

God wants us to have the kind of attitude that says, "Wherever you take me, Lord, I'll go. Whatever you ask me to do, I'll do. I trust you with every part of my life!" Abraham had this kind of deep faith, and God richly blessed him because of it.

He showed His Heavenly Father the depth of his love and commitment to Him through his willingness to obey God when he was instructed to sacrifice his son, Isaac. The Lord didn't really want his child as a sacrifice, just Abraham's willingness to obey! He spared the boy and told his father to instead offer the ram that was caught in a thicket nearby.

Then, He revealed to Abraham that He would bless him abundantly for having such a yielded heart. Genesis 22:17-18 declares:

> ...blessing I will bless you, and multiplying
> I will multiply your descendants as the stars
> of the heaven and as the sand which is on the
> seashore; and your descendants shall possess
> the gate of their enemies. In your seed all the
> nations of the earth shall be blessed, because
> you have obeyed My voice.

In these passages, we find a perfect example of how God blesses us when we choose to obey, rather than giving in to fear when Satan tempts us to trust him instead through fearfully erected coping mechanisms. Our Heavenly Father desires to abundantly shower us with His blessings. Hebrews 6:13-20 declares:

> For when God made a promise to Abraham...
> saying 'Surely blessing I will bless you, and
> multiplying I will multiply you.' And so,
> after he had patiently endured, he obtained
> the promise... Thus God, determining to
> show more <u>abundantly</u> to the heirs of promise
> ... confirmed it by an oath... in which it is
> impossible for God to lie, we might have
> strong consolation, who have fled for refuge to
> lay hold of the hope set before us. [Emphasis
> author's]
>
> This hope we have as an anchor of the soul,
> both sure and steadfast...

In the same manner in which this mighty man of God received the Lord's promise of an abundant life we, too, can experience the same thing. Because of Jesus' sacrifice, we have now become the "heirs of promise," as was Abraham. We're entitled to receive the same blessings, but they're conditional upon us being willing to love, honor and obey the Lord and to find our refuge in Him.

A HEALTHY MAN OR WOMAN PUTS AWAY CHILDISH THINGS

We have much reason to be hopeful. Don't expect, however, that once you choose to live for Jesus with your whole heart that everything will get easier. In fact, in many cases, you can expect circumstances to grow worse before they get better! Why? Because Satan will use every weapon in his arsenal to convince you that life was easier when you were in prison—when you embraced a survival rather than a revival mindset.

When I think of negative coping mechanisms and, specifically, blaming, Carroll O'Connor's role as Archie Bunker in the *All in the Family* series that ran from 1971-1979 comes to mind. Archie was a frustrated, blue collar worker who was stuck in a dead-end job. He was very opinionated, uneducated and embraced many negative stereotypes about different races and political groups. [5] He often displaced his anger on innocent people. He blamed his wife, Edith, played by Jean Stapleton, for almost everything and she was so compliant and co-dependent that she even apologized for the bad weather!

Archie was also an equal opportunity discriminator. He blamed the world's problems on Democrats, Jews, Roman Catholics, African-Americans, Hispanics, Italians, and Polish people, to name just a few. And when his son-in-law, Michael, played by Rob Reiner, confronted Archie on his racist views, he was quick to call Michael all kinds of insulting names. Archie gave him the nickname "Meathead" to mock his intelligence and especially for standing up for minorities. [6]

Archie was heavily into blaming and allowed the desires of his flesh to run wild. This is probably what made him so comical, since he literally had no control of his mouth. As funny as this comedy was, the sad reality is that some people never grow up and stay stuck in a stereotypical, blaming mindset until the day they die.

Listen to the Apostle Paul's words of wisdom in 1 Corinthians 13:11, "When I was a child, I spoke as a child, I understood as a child, I thought as a child; but when I became a man, I put away childish things." No one can do it for you; you must make the choice to let go of the fearful, childish ways of protecting yourself and blaming others. You must make the choice to allow Jesus into your darkest, hidden places and to heal your wounded spirit. He won't be surprised at what He finds there; in fact, He already knows all about it. Go ahead and be honest with Him.

God can take away your pain. Tell Him that you're angry, bitter or afraid—He already knows that, too! He wants you to bare your heart to Him because He loves you! What greater freedom could there be than knowing that what Jesus spoke was true in John 8:32?—"And you shall know the truth, and the truth shall make you free." It's time to grow up emotionally, my friend.

It is time to face the truth: will you continue to dwell in fear, or will you choose to dwell in the House of the Lord?

PERSONAL INVENTORY OF NEGATIVE COPING MECHANISMS

Here is a list of some of the most common mind-games that people draw from in an effort to protect themselves. This is an opportunity for you to examine how often you allow fear to control you. Check how many behaviors you habitually use. If you really want a clear picture of where you stand, let someone you love and trust examine this list with you.

_____Lying: Deliberately not telling the truth with the intent of deceiving others. This includes broken promises, flattery, cheating on your taxes, allowing others to have a false impression of you or your accomplishments, or something as simple as keeping the extra money when a store employee makes a mistake in your favor.

_____Denial: Pretending a problem does not exist.

_____Minimizing: Trying to convince ourselves or others that the situation is not that bad ("Just one more drink won't hurt" or "If I sin just this once, God will forgive me").

_____Maximizing: Blowing something way out of proportion, exaggerating, or boasting.

_____Rationalizing: Attributing our behaviors, opinions, etc., to causes or reasons that seem valid but are, in fact, not true ("I can't afford to get up too early to pray because I need my sleep," when, in actuality, one simply chooses not to make prayer a priority).

_____Bargaining: Attempting to manipulate God or others

by promising a certain behavior in order to get something that you want ("God, if you'll get me out of this mess, I promise that I'll do anything You ask...").

_____Manipulating: Using guilt, tears, anger or even "smooth talk" to get what we want from others ("If you really loved me, you would do what I want").

_____Excessive humor: Joking a large amount of the time in order to not have to face a painful situation, or continuing to make fun of someone through teasing or by making someone the brunt of a joke.

_____Intellectualizing: Expressing what we think, rather than how we feel, as a means of avoiding a painful situation.

_____Excessive television watching: Vegetating in front of the television for hours so we don't have to face emotional hurts in our lives.

_____Tuning others out/withdrawing: Choosing to ignore others when we're not interested in them, are bored, or don't want to listen to what they have to say.

_____Self-punishment: Abusing ourselves by refusing to do things which are necessary for good, physical or mental health, or by negative self-talk ("I don't deserve to be happy, so I won't eat" or "I'm a failure—I'll never amount to anything good").

_____Avoiding: Constantly reacting to a problem by changing the subject, or by saying, "I don't want to talk about it right now." This is similar to denial, but avoiding includes going out of one's way to not see the person with whom we have a conflict.

_____Defensiveness: Reacting sharply and aggressively when confronted by someone ("What do you mean I have a problem with my temper?").

_____Excessive sarcasm: Using sneering or cutting remarks the majority of the time to express the opposite of what we mean.

_____Saying that we don't care: Choosing not to openly admit that we care about a person or topic in order to protect our feelings ("I don't care whether my dad says that he loves me or not; I don't need him!").

_____Giving someone the "silent treatment": Refusing to speak with someone when we're upset with a certain individual as a result of unresolved anger, fear, or a desire for revenge.

_____Catastrophizing: Constantly imagining that the worst possible thing is going to happen in a specific situation.

_____Worrying: Feeling uneasy, anxious, or tormenting ourselves with disturbing thoughts about a situation over which we have no control; a form of fear which shows that we are afraid that circumstances won't turn out the way that we want them to.

_____Laziness: Avoiding work and responsibilities; a form of denial that includes procrastination, complacency, and sometimes a fear that one won't measure up to someone else's expectations.

_____Busyness: Being overly caught up in one's job, church or leisure activities in order to avoid having to face emotional pain. This is another form of denial which manifests itself through refusal to be alone or to have time for quiet contemplation.

_____Being critical and negative: Continually criticizing or putting others down by pointing out their faults in an attempt to make ourselves look better.

_____Making excuses: Constantly justifying failures instead of admitting our mistakes.

_____Being vengeful: holding a grudge toward someone rather than forgiving him, thinking that we are punishing that person when, in fact, we are hurting ourselves.

_____Blaming: Putting others at fault rather than assuming personal responsibility.

_____Perfectionism: Striving for the highest degree of excellence, skill and proficiency, at any cost, including one's own health and the destruction of one's relationships with others. Demanding perfection from self or others is the goal one strives for, regardless of the casualties suffered along the way.

_____Spreading rumors/gossiping: Talking badly about someone with whom we are angry as a means of hurting them back or as a means of making ourselves look better.

_____Causing physical injury: Hitting, kicking or slapping someone as a means of settling a conflict.

_____Character assassination: Verbally abusing someone through name-calling, swearing or ridicule to the point that it causes mental and emotional harm.

_____Swearing: Using profanity, whether it is spoken or unspoken (under one's breath).

_____Putting on a mask: Pretending to be something or someone that we're really not (putting on a smile or happy face when we're really feeling sad or upset or saying we feel fine when we really don't feel fine).

_____Condescending: Talking down to others or patronizing to make others look inferior.

_____Intellectual assassination or superiority: Using elitist vocabulary (big, high-sounding words) to make others look inferior in comparison.

_____Dabbling in the occult: Using the occult (tarot cards, channeling, Ouija boards, astrology, etc.) as a means to gain control of circumstances or of others.

Some of the more destructive survival behaviors include smoking, substance abuse and eating disorders. Other deviant disorders include promiscuity, pornography, stealing and suicidal ideation. Many people also join gangs or cults in an effort to cope and find an alternative family system when they feel that the Lord and/or their families have failed to accept them.

This is precisely why God warns us to repent now and turn from our wicked ways while there is still breath in us. He wants us to become part of His family now because once we die we won't have any more opportunities to get right with Him. Hebrews 9:27 soberly reminds us that "...it is appointed for men to die once, but after this the judgment."

If you've been honest with yourself and you've checked many of the above behaviors, don't despair! Jesus is able to deliver you from every one of them! In fact, you've already taken the first step to freedom: you've acknowledged your sin. Congratulations, my friend! God highly values your honesty.

WILL YOU DWELL IN FEAR, OR IN IN THE HOUSE OF THE LORD?

As you go on, My child, with the life that you lead,
The condition of your heart you must examine.
Are you a blooming flower or a tumbleweed
That's tossed in the desert and knows only famine?

Do you build walls to protect you from caring friends?
Do you dress up to look good for appearance's sake?
Beware, lest your devices destroy you in the end:
The silent pain that you carry is the enemy's bait.

Denial, minimizing and rationalizing
Arose when Adam and Eve tasted of the forbidden fruit.
This led to lying, stealing, and manipulating:
Evils that joined forces with poisonous roots.

How long have you lived behind an invisible shield
Which protects the feelings you need to lay out on a table?
This deadly self-made fortress in which you are sealed
Reveals your darkened heart; the condition you've enabled.

Allow God to deliver you from hatred, guilt, and shame.
Be open, honest, and heed His heavenly call.
Abandon the lie that you've lived and the poison it contains,
And allow Him to enter your prison and tear down your walls.

His Son declared, "I am the resurrection and the life.
He who believes in Me, though he were dead, yet shall he live."
Shed your graveclothes of despair that have cut you like a knife,
Allow Jesus to heal your wounds through the grace that He
    gives.

By not trusting God to heal your hurts you call Him a liar,
Yet, He came to give life so you can have it more abundantly.
Jesus came to rescue you from the enemy's filth and mire,
Which has prevented you from declaring: "I'm finally free!"

God says, "I'll remove the stony heart that has hardened your
ways And give you a fleshy heart as a testimony of My love.
The eternal well you'll draw from will bless you all of your days
Through the same Spirit that descended to My Son as a dove.

You must live a resurrected life and put away childish things.
Exchange your lies for the truth and do away with just surviving.
You are an heir of promise: Rest under the shadow of My
    wings!
Approach My throne for healing, for it's you whom I'm
    reviving.

Receive the courage that I have for you to face your hidden pain.
Trust Jesus as the Hope of Glory and Anchor of your soul.
Yield your spirit in thanksgiving and glorify My name:
With healing I will touch your life as you surrender all control.

As you learn to love Me, I'll remove all fear that you own.
The enemy that you've listened to seldom bites but often roars.
Decide now, My beloved, as you approach My holy throne:
Will you dwell in fear or in the House of the Lord?"

CHAPTER TWO

BECOMING THE BRIDE OF CHRIST

"...as the bridegroom rejoices over the bride,
so shall your God rejoice
over you"
(Isaiah 62:5)

It is a scene often repeated in old movies: two young lovers rush to embrace from opposite ends of a flower-filled field. Deliriously in love, they run toward each other with arms outstretched, completely oblivious to anything or anyone else. Then, when they finally meet, they throw themselves into an ecstatic embrace, rejoicing in the purity and devotion of their love for one another.

With this image in mind, read Isaiah 62:5 again: "...as the bridegroom rejoices over the bride, so shall your God rejoice over you" [emphasis author's]. This is the fulfillment of God's creation, the purpose for your very existence: "And you shall love the Lord your God with all your heart, with all your soul, with all your mind, and with all your strength..." (Mark 12:30).

All the good works, all the gifts to charity, and all the time spent devoted to ministry are only secondary in God's eyes to what He wants most from us—our hearts! What He desires above all else is that His passionate, infinite love for each of us be returned unto Him with the same kind of fervor. This is the true goal of every believer: to discover the joy of falling in love and being completely in love with Jesus!

TRUSTING GOD TO BE YOUR BRIDEGROOM

No matter what gut-wrenching tragedies or agonizing memories may haunt us from the past, God has promised that He will not give up on us; indeed, there is abundant life available to us! Everyone bears lacerations on their hearts from broken relationships that need tending to because no one is immune from the evil of our day. As violence and abuse are glorified on television screens, on our streets, in our schools and in numerous households throughout our nation, we must remember that, as Christians, we are impacted, too.

Matthew 5:45 soberly reminds us that "…He makes His sun rise on the evil and the good, and sends rain on the just and the unjust." We all carry battle scars and often fresh wounds that still pierce our souls. Our wounds, however, are no excuse for not serving God or for not trusting Him as our Bridegroom.

Can you imagine two people marrying who do not trust each other, or where one person is trustworthy, but the other is not? Unfortunately, this happens much too often from what I've observed in my life experiences and in the professional counseling that I've provided to troubled people. But what kind of marriage or romantic relationship do these people have?

In such an arrangement, there is no real intimacy, no true friendship, no security, and inevitably, no love! This is not what the Lord intended, neither for earthly marriages and dating relationships nor for our relationship with Him. The bottom line: we must learn to trust God completely and without wavering in all aspects of our lives.

Unfortunately, when we've been betrayed, this is easier said than done. But when we fully realize that the One to whom we must surrender everything is totally in love with us and desires only the best for us, how much easier it becomes to rest in His presence. For it is by the glory of His grace that we've been given "…everlasting consolation and good hope…" (2 Thessalonians 2:16) and "…by which He has made us accepted in the Beloved" (Ephesians 1:6).

WHAT DOES IT MEAN TO BE THE BRIDE OF CHRIST?

Do you remember when you were engaged to your future spouse and were planning your wedding? Just the thought of your fiancée would cause your face to light up and prompt you to envision your future together. For you, men, God was fulfilling His promise to bless you with the beautiful princess of your dreams! And for you, women, this was the special, handsome prince that you had prayed for, waited for, hoped for and longed for.

With this mind, does it seem strange to realize that Jesus

also prays, hopes, longs and waits for you? He delights to spend time with you and His face lights up with joy at the thought of you! Zephaniah 3:16-17 proclaims,

> …Do not fear; Zion, let not your hands be weak. The Lord your God in your midst, The Mighty One, will save; He will rejoice over you with gladness, He will quiet you with His love, He will rejoice over you with singing.

Through a word-study of the Hebrew, listen to the depth of expression communicated by the original text:

> Do not let anyone make you afraid or frighten you, daughter of Zion. Don't let your hands cease or slacken from the task: do not faint, become feeble or slothful in what I have called you to do. The Self-Existent, Eternal God is within you, in your very heart; He is a Powerful Warrior, your Champion Who is strong and valiant. He will cause you to be free and safe; He will avenge, defend, deliver, help, preserve and rescue you, and bring your salvation and victory! He will be greatly glad and make mirth over you with exceeding gladness, pleasure and rejoicing! He will cause you to be quiet and rest from all of your worries and petitions by His great love. He will spin around and leap for joy over you with shouts of joy, cries of gladness and songs of triumph.

If you're married, think back to your wedding day: how wonderful it was to love so completely and so passionately, to know that your bethrothed had chosen to give him or herself solely to you! The joy that radiated from your relationship must have been contagious, and all of your close friends must have known exactly of whom you were thinking when "that look" flashed across your face. People in love have every reason to be joyful.

Similarly, <u>when we dedicated our lives to Christ</u>, <u>Jesus</u>

took us in His arms and loved us like no one ever had before! God, Himself, has chosen us to be His beloved! Just as you eagerly anticipated seeing your lovely, glowing bride dressed all in white or your fine-looking, irresistible groom decked out in striking attire, so does God eagerly await His Wedding Day.

Even though it has become common and accepted nowadays to see brides who are not virgins wearing white, the traditional wedding dress is supposed to signify purity, integrity and moral excellence. The Lord's Bride will be pure in every respect! This applies to the man and woman who are dedicated to the Lord. Uncontaminated from other lovers, both will be worthy to wear white because they've chosen not to hide anything from their blessed Redeemer. God's true believers are firm and unfailing in their allegiance to God because they have their eyes on their Beloved: Jesus! Nothing could delight Him more!

FALLING IN LOVE WITH CHRIST

Do you reminisce about God in the same way that two lovers daydream about each other? They love everything about one another. They memorize one another's physical features because they don't want to forget anything about their sweetheart when they're apart. Even when they're separated, all they can think about is being together again. They long to embrace and gently touch one another. They yearn to hold one another's hand and when they kiss, they experience sheer ecstasy because they know this is a special love they've reserved solely for each other.

Serving Christ throughout our lives should be no different. Becoming born-again is the most joyous time we'll ever experience here on earth, even more so than our earthly wedding day. This is because receiving Christ as our Lord and Savior means deliverance from our rebellious lifestyles, forgiveness for all of our sins, and the promise of being with the Lord one day forever in Heaven. Our love union with Jesus began when we asked Him to come into our hearts through the power of the Holy Spirit. If we're truly sincere in our walks with the Lord, this is the beginning of a love relationship that will never end.

If this does not cause us to be excited and hopeful, then

perhaps we've fallen out of touch with what being born-again encompasses and have instead embraced a dead religion. If you aren't thrilled about fellowshipping with God through the avenue of prayer, perhaps you've been sucked in by a lie. Perhaps you've been drawn in by religious tradition rather than Jesus Himself. God is not boring. He is alive and very much in love with you!

Jesus loved each of us so much that He came to live among us, died for us, rose from the dead, blessed us with the Holy Spirit who desires to dwell inside of us, and has given us the promise of eternal life. This should be more than enough to cause us to celebrate with jubilant singing and dancing, even as David did when he danced unashamedly before the Lord with all his might (2 Samuel 6:14).

THE BRIDE MUST WAIT PATIENTLY FOR HER GROOM

However, it is true that as the Bride of Christ, we face a formidable struggle in keeping our flame of love brightly burning. Matthew 24:12-13 says, "And because lawlessness will abound, the love of many will grow cold. But he who endures [in loving Christ] to the end shall be saved." The excitement and fulfillment that come from loving God through obeying the Holy Spirit will waste away if we choose to stop seeking Him for direction. We'll cease from growing spiritually if we don't drink daily from His well of living water (John 4:1-13).

Lawlessness is skyrocketing at an alarming rate in our world. What was completely unacceptable and even unthinkable less than fifty years ago (the legalization of marihuana, cohabitation and rampant divorce) is commonplace today—but God's moral standards do not change. If we fail to stay close to our Lord, we'll fall into compromise and our hearts will grow cold.

The enemy of our souls doesn't want us to make it to the Wedding Day. He'll do everything within his power to see that we aren't present at the Marriage Supper of the Lamb. A true servant of the Lord, however, will not be intimidated by the ploys of the enemy because he's focused on taking hold of the Prize that awaits every believer who overcomes: Jesus standing with open arms waiting to receive him or her into glory and proclaiming, "Well done, My good and faithful servant. Enter now into the joy of your reward!"

What could be more fulfilling than living a virtuous life and knowing that Jesus will reward us one day by allowing us to spend eternity with Him? Nothing. Absolutely nothing! What an honor and a privilege that will be. The marriage ceremony between a husband and wife is only a foreshadowing of the day of celebration when Jesus Christ will be reunited with His Bride—all true followers of Christ.

WHERE ARE YOU IN YOUR LEVEL OF COMMITMENT TO GOD?

How can we gauge where we are in our love relationship with Christ? It isn't difficult to do a personal inventory. We either make time to be with the Lord or we don't. If we choose not to commune with God regularly, we neglect the most important aspect of our lives: our spiritual condition. If we fail to fellowship with the Lord and don't seek healthy, meaningful relationships with other believers, we slowly waste away. Proverbs 27:17 reminds us that "As iron sharpens iron, so a man [or woman] sharpens the countenance of his [or her] friend."

Marriage is no different. If we fail to spend time communicating with our spouses, our marriage will wither up and gradually die. In fact, the two relationships are intertwined; as our prayer lives begin to erode, so do the freshness and vitality that were once present in our marriage. Prayer produces fuel for a healthy marriage or a pure dating relationship. It ushers in unconditional love straight from God's throne-room, which enables us to love our spouse or beloved dating partner as Christ loves His Church (Ephesians 5:25).

Along the same lines, if we fail to put gasoline in our vehicle, the tank will eventually run dry and the engine will stop running. If we fail to pay our utility bill, the electric company will shut off the power to our homes. If we don't eat healthy food, our bodies will weaken and eventually shut down. And if we fail to water our garden, our fruits and vegetables will wither up and die. God has given us plenty of physical examples of this spiritual truth: there must always be fresh fuel (prayer) in our gas tanks (hearts) so that our walk with the Lord and our relationship with our spouse and loved ones will remain wholesome, healthy and meaningful.

Why are we so surprised when our marriage or romantic relationship grows cold? The Holy Spirit desires to continually fuel our special dating relationship, but if we fail to ask Him for love and wisdom in how to bless our partner, then our romantic overtures will grow stale and he or she will feel neglected and rejected rather than cherished and protected. It's our responsibility to ask the Helper (John 14:16-17) daily to fill us afresh with His new anointing so we can remain passionately in love with Jesus and our spouse or future helpmate.

Ruth Ward Heflin talks about this in her book, *Glory: Experiencing the Atmosphere of Heaven:*

> If your relationship with your husband is one in which he makes the living, he takes out the garbage, he drives the car, he does certain errands, then it's not much of a relationship. That happens with many marriages. It is a "verb" relationship, based on what he does.
>
> Many husbands, in turn, say of their wives, "She is a wonderful cook. She keeps the house clean. She cares for the children." Before you were married, did she cook the meals? Did she clean the house? Did she take care of the kids? What was it that made you love her?
>
> "Well, it was those blue eyes." Have you forgotten she still has those blue eyes?
>
> "Well, it was that smile." Have you forgotten that she still has that smile?...Women forget what made them fall in love with their husbands, too.
>
> "Oh, it was the way he stood. There was just something about him. I could feel his

strength." That was the way she thought of him before they were married. Afterwards she thinks only of what he does. He thinks only of what she does.

It is the same in our relationship with the Lord. When we first met Him, He hadn't done anything for us that we were aware of. But we saw that He was wonderful.

"Oh, I love Him with all my heart," new converts are prone to say. After we're saved a while, we think about Him in a different way: "He saved me. He filled me with the Holy Ghost. He heals me when I'm sick." But what about Him as a <u>person</u>?.. If we fell in love with Him, not knowing Him, shouldn't knowing Him bring a greater relationship of love and worship? [7]

When we were courting, we did everything possible to please our sweetheart to make ourselves irresistible. If prayer kept you in love when you were dating the one you found so desirable, prayer will keep you in love as you persevere in your marriage or courting experience. Just don't forget that this spiritual principle works both ways. God wooed and romanced us into His loving arms when He saved us from eternal damnation because His presence was irresistible. Our hearts will only remain loving and joyful for as long as we draw from the fuel that comes directly from the Lord through the avenue of prayer.

If we neglect the Holy Spirit, everything we touch will run dry. This includes our hearts, our marriage or dating relationship, our children, and our ministry. God and his gift of a marriage or romantic partner were never meant to be ignored. One day we'll have to give an account to the Lord for our relationship with Him and for how we treated our spouse and loved ones.

ARE YOU A WISE OR A FOOLISH VIRGIN?

In the parable of the wise and foolish virgins in Matthew 25:1-13, Jesus tells a story about five foolish virgins who went to a wedding feast unprepared because their lamps had no oil and, as a result, were not allowed to enter. Jesus also gives an example of five wise, virtuous women whose lanterns were filled and who were prepared to meet the Lord. Verse 13 states, "Watch therefore, for you know neither the day nor the hour in which the Son of Man is coming."

Jesus reminds us that, as the Bride of Christ, we must always be prepared to meet the Lord. Why? Because He could return at any time! Our lamps must overflow with the fresh outpouring of the Holy Spirit, meaning we need to commune with our loving Lord regularly.

The virgins with empty lanterns represent those who have neglected God in their lives. Just as each woman was responsible for making sure that her lantern was filled, every believer has a responsibility to stay free from the world's contaminants. We cannot be spiritually lazy and expect to be made virtuous because of someone else's efforts.

When we stand before the Lord after we die, there will be no one else on whom we can lean for support. No one else can loan us some of their oil for our lamp. Only by consistently being with our Fiancé through prayer will we be able to present ourselves as a pure, fully-committed, spotless Bride when we go to live with Jesus for eternity.

Before this grand event takes place, however, we'll face numerous trials where we'll either deny or acknowledge to the world that we know the Lord. Jesus declared in Matthew 10:32-33 that "whoever confesses Me before men, him I will also confess before My Father who is in Heaven. But whoever denies Me before men, him I will also deny before My Father who is in Heaven."

A Christian who is truly committed to loving Jesus is not timid or fearful when it comes to sharing God's love with others. He's ready at all times to testify of Christ because He trusts the Holy Spirit to give him courage over fear of ridicule, persecution, torture or even death. As the Bride of

Christ we should always be ready to joyfully testify about how the Lord has loved us, set us free from sin and enabled us to love others through His bountiful grace.

We're reminded in 1 Peter 3:15 about the significance of sharing our faith. It states, "But sanctify the Lord God, and always be ready to give a defense to everyone who asks you a reason for the hope that is in you, with meekness and fear [reverence towards God]." At the same time, Colossians 1:27-28 reminds us that "...Christ [is] in you, the Hope of Glory: whom we preach, warning every man, and teaching every man in all wisdom; that we may present every man perfect in Christ Jesus."

THE FOOLISH VIRGINS— COMMITTED TO THEMSELVES

Unfortunately, some people whom I've counseled have a mistaken notion that grace means they can still do whatever they want following their self-proclaimed conversion to Christ as if they were divinely given a free license to sin. They continue in their immoral lifestyles without genuine remorse. They have no desire to make necessary character changes because they love their sins too much. They're unwilling to completely cut soul ties with their wayward past.

These people want God's forgiveness, but not the self-denial that includes giving up their worldly ways. Though their hearts are not fully devoted to God, they believe the Lord will one day allow them to enter into Heaven in their present, corrupt states as the Bride of Christ. But I ask, will God accept as His Bride one who is sullied and corrupted with other lovers? The answer is a resounding "No!"

Even though people can be fooled, God knows whether we pray the sinner's prayer with sincerity or insincerity. He knows the difference between lip-service and true conversion. Anyone can go through the motions of asking Jesus to come into their lives without a true desire to serve Him or to live a holy life for Him but God sees right through our motives. <u>If our heart is not honest, then there is no genuine conversion to Christ and our words merely fall to the ground</u>.

Revelation 21:27 reveals that "…there shall by no means enter it [Heaven]anything that defiles, or causes an abomination or a lie, but only those whose names are written in the Lamb's Book of Life" [emphasis author's]. A truly converted person will have evidence that He lived for the Lord through his actions. James 2:20 supports this concept, "But do you want to know, O foolish man, that faith without works is dead?" James expounds on this further in verse 24 by clarifying "…that a man is justified by works, and not by faith only." Yes, we receive salvation through faith but our works (our service to God out of our love for Him) prove over time that our conversion experience was genuine.

Beware: even if someone prophesies, sings magnificently in the choir or preaches the gospel passionately, that in and of itself does not mean one's heart is right with the Lord. How can we know if an individual is not using his spiritual gift with selfish motives where he's drawing attention to himself rather than glorifying the Lord? Only God knows our hearts, but we must always be discerning of what is happening around us in the spiritual realm so we aren't deceived. This is our responsibility.

And just because someone operates in power with astounding signs and wonders does not necessarily mean that the Lord endorses that individual or their ministry. These are all outward manifestations by which we judge people, but God judges us by the extent to which we are yielded to Him. He cares greatly about how surrendered we are in allowing Him to transform us more into the image of Christ.

After having spoken with many "foolish virgins" on a personal and professional counseling level, I realized over time that "justified" to them does not mean "made righteous or found innocent by God." [8] To the contrary, it translates into "rationalizing." This is the same sin that Adam and Eve fell to when they allowed themselves to be deceived in the Garden.

These people have not been transformed by Christ, but are led by their own carnal minds because they haven't severed ties with this world. Many are still heavily entrenched in evil, yet active in church to help them cope with their guilt. They live a double life. Striving to live an abundant life in the Lord is the farthest thing from their minds. They still believe they're justified in their ungodly manner of living and are deceived in believing that God will one day receive them into glory in their present carnal condition.

I've also met several of these people while street-witnessing. Despite their alcohol and drug habits, they claimed, "I'm going to Heaven because I prayed the sinner's prayer. There's nothing else I have to do." They even boldly declare, "I have my eternal fire insurance." They are deceived! Either some believer gave them only part of God's truth or they misinterpreted the salvation message or they practiced selective hearing where they only took to heart what they wanted to hear.

The Lord Himself declares in Revelation 3:16, "So then, because you are lukewarm, and neither cold nor hot, I will vomit you out of My mouth." God can't be fooled. He knows our hearts and which people are serious about living holy lives and which individuals are not interested in pursuing purity.

To illustrate, I talked with someone recently who said she was a Bible instructor for many years, faithfully took her children to church services on Sundays and Bible studies on Wednesday nights, but said she stopped participating in organized religion years ago because it became too legalistic—too many rules and regulations. Now, she claims to still be a born-again, spirit-filled Christian and says she loves Jesus, but openly claims to be a nudist.

This reminds me of a commercial that I watched as a child where the television announcer was encouraging a woman to express her true self as he kept saying "Come on baby, let it all hang out." In this case, it's not only unfortunate but tragic when a person exposes oneself (literally) with no concern for how it will affect other people, and especially children. This is, quite frankly, absolute carnality and outright selfishness coupled with a lack of self-respect and respect for others.

When in doubt, we must remember that humility, by far, surpasses narcissism. We please God when we exercise good judgment. And when our flesh does not want to cooperate, we simply need to tell it to "Shut up and obey the Word of God!" We need to quickly show our carnal nature who's the boss before we suffer loss. Listen to what the Lord has to say about this issue through the Apostle Paul in 1 Corinthians 9:27: "But I buffet my body and bring it into subjection, lest, when I have preached to others, I myself should become disqualified."

The reason why public nudity is wrong is because we're encouraged in God's Word to avoid not just evil, but the appearance of evil (1 Thessalonians 5:22). Since we live in such a corrupt world, I don't believe a man can look at a beautiful, naked woman or a woman look at a handsome, nude man for long before they begin to lust after one another. Nudity (and sexual oneness, for that matter) between a man and a woman is reserved strictly for marriage, just as God designed it.

Genesis 2:25 reminds us that Adam and Eve were the first married couple in the following passage, "And they were both naked, the man and his wife, and were not ashamed." This is the only time in the Bible that the Lord condones mutual nakedness and oneness without shame between a man and a woman—in a marital relationship. He does not condone sexual intimacy in cohabitation arrangements, in extramarital affairs, in premarital sexual relationships (regardless of whether two people love each other and plan to marry one another), in motion pictures, the internet or nudist camps.

I can't find any exceptions to this directive and if you don't believe me, re-read Genesis 2:25 and research other cross references. I guarantee you that you won't find any loopholes. That's because God was very clear in His instructions to us about sexual purity in order to guard us against unnecessary heartache and suffering and so we could maintain a holy relationship with the Lord.

We always need to be thinking about how our conduct affects not just us, but other people, too, since Jesus has called us to love our neighbor as ourselves (Mark 12:31). This is the heart of the Gospel. And holiness is of the essence because the Lord proclaims in Matthew 5:8 that "Blessed are the pure in heart, for they shall see God."

Had I been faced with this woman's dilemma, I would have re-examined my relationship with Christ to see if I was falling into a works-mentality where one is trying to please God through good works or religious tradition rather than spiritual intimacy. I would have also met with my pastor to talk about these concerns regarding the church she was attending to resolve this dilemma. If that didn't work, then, I would have prayed and asked the Lord to lead me to another congregation.

But, to wind up a nudist obviously shows that this woman completely missed the mark and was utterly deceived, especially since she totally fell out of fellowship with other believers (Hebrews 10:25). It's also possible that this wayward soul was simply looking to fulfill the wild desires of her flesh and, in order to do so, she had to rationalize an excuse for leaving her faith.

People sometimes choose to turn their backs on God because their flesh is stronger than their spirit. Their failure to cultivate a strong prayer and devotional life points to spiritual negligence and will cause anyone to fall away from the Lord in a hurry. I'm not saying that they did not experience a true conversion to Christ because they may very well have.

It could be that their prayer lives decayed or they fell into a stagnant, spiritual routine, rather than keeping their devotional lives fresh. It's also possible that they were exposed to temptation until it sucked them in, became a secret sin and eventually a lifestyle that tore them away from their faith. If they were true believers, hopefully, once they hit rock bottom, like the prodigal son (Luke 15:11-32), they'll be wooed back by the Holy Spirit when they grow more desperate for deliverance from their depravity.

Other people have experienced an awakening in their lives, but no true transformation, and have become more aware of what the spiritual realm encompasses by simply being around Christians, attending church services, and witnessing the power of the Holy Spirit transform others. After all, in the parable of the wise and foolish virgins (Matthew 25:1-13), the foolish virgins were waiting for the Groom. They apparently had heard about Jesus and knew He was coming.

Their modern counterparts may even talk and act like practicing Christians, but they're not (see Matthew 7:15-16) because they have no depth of relationship or desire to live a pure life that's pleasing to the Lord. They still love (or should I say, lust after) their sin because they have not allowed God to love them in such a way that they would be willing to forsake their old ways of survival. They're not done partying with the world yet. Hopefully, they'll be enlightened to the point of conversion before their life ends.

Ephesians 5:27 reminds us that Christ is coming back for a glorious church without spot or wrinkle. He is returning for a holy church, without blemish or fears! Here, God is talking about a healthy church that doesn't play any mind-games; one that doesn't try to run and hide from Him, but one that runs to Him whenever evil tries to overcome them.

The foolish virgins may believe with their minds that they are saved, but they don't believe it with their hearts. People who are involved in ministry and hide rather than repent of their secret sins are deceived by evil influence and led astray. Listen to the judgment that awaits them as Jesus reveals in Matthew 7:21-23,

> Not everyone who says to Me, "Lord, Lord,"
> shall enter the kingdom of Heaven, but he
> who does the will of My Father in Heaven.
> Many will say to Me in that day, "Lord, Lord,
> have we not prophesied in Your name, cast
> out demons in Your name, and done many
> wonders in Your name?" And then I will
> declare to them, "I never knew you; depart
> from Me, you who practice lawlessness!"

God is very interested in having a special relationship with us more than anything else. For that reason alone, we need to be on our guard against false doctrines that may lead us astray. Paul expounds on this in 2 Corinthians 11:2-4,

> For I am jealous for you with godly jealousy.
> For I have betrothed you to one husband, that
> I may present you as a chaste virgin to Christ.

But I fear, lest somehow, as the serpent
deceived Eve by his craftiness, so your minds
may be corrupted from the simplicity that is in
Christ. For if he who comes preaches another
Jesus whom we have not preached, or if you
receive a different spirit which you have not
received, or a different gospel which you have
not accepted, you may well put up with it.

At this point, you may want to turn back to the list
of coping behaviors at the end of chapter one. Do you
recognize any of them as sins which are preventing you from
completely surrendering to Jesus? For instance, the sin of
complacency—being satisfied with where you are spiritually
or emotionally (especially if you tend to stuff rather than
face your pain) is just as deadly as the sin of murder (though
both have different consequences here on earth). Why?
Because in the same manner in which a murderer refuses
to acknowledge the value of human life by killing another
person, you can kill yourself spiritually by allowing pride to
prevent you from repenting of sin.

In essence, you, like the murderer, refuse to
acknowledge the value that the Lord places on human life
and, in this case, yours! Remember: a hurt that you attempt
to hide from yourself, God, or others becomes a sin when
you allow pride to keep you from facing it. Satan would be
delighted to keep you locked in the snare of these destructive
defense mechanisms while he deceives you into thinking that
you're really free—free to sin, that is.

It is for this reason that the Lord so strongly
encourages all of us throughout His Word to seek wisdom,
understanding and discernment: so we may recognize those
other "suitors" who would attempt to steal us away from
our Betrothed: Jesus. Just as infidelity is devastating to a
marriage or even an engagement, a roving heart will destroy
our intimacy with the Lord. The good news is that when we
maintain a daily level of intimate communion with Jesus, the
more we put to death the evil desires that once enslaved us!

The more time we spend with the Lord, the more we
get to know and love Him and the more we desire to please

Him by obeying His admonition to live a holy life.
In John 14:15 Jesus clearly stated, "If you love Me, keep
My commandments." If we're truly committed to Christ,
we'll do all we can to keep our hearts pure. The Bride of
Christ keeps herself free from the stain of sin through her
love for her Groom. Do you? If not, you can start today!

THE WISE VIRGINS—COMMITTED TO CHRIST UNTIL DEATH

I once heard a pastor share a story of born-again,
Russian Christians who were meeting secretly in their
homeland for prayer meetings. They were faithful to
meet regularly to praise and worship the Lord, despite the
possibility of death if the secret police found out about it.
On one night, after each believer had arrived to the prayer
service, a loud pounding was heard at the door, "Open up!
This is the KGB (Russian spy agency)!"

Suddenly, fear gripped their hearts, for they knew
the penalty for meeting to pray meant torture, imprisonment
or death. After hesitating, the doors were opened and the
secret police stormed their way through. The two men who
entered were armed with machine guns. They demanded to
know what the assembly was about. Immediately, a believer
announced they were having a prayer service and honoring
their Christian God.

After a few moments of stunned silence, the KGB
agents shouted, "Anyone who chooses to leave now will not
face any consequences. But you must renounce your faith
in God and agree to not attend any more prayer meetings."
Four people quickly left the room.

Then, a final proclamation was made for anyone else
who wished to deny their faith. Two more people rushed
out. At that point, the tension mounted as the armed men
locked the doors from the inside so that no one could get in
or out. The remaining men, women and children refused to
reject their faith in the One and Only Living God who meant
everything to them. They were prepared to die for Him.

Shockingly, the agents suddenly disclosed, "We are
also devout followers of Jesus Christ and would like to know
if we can join you in your prayer meeting?" Not only were

these faithful believers relieved but it was revealed which people were truly not committed to Christ when they realized it could cost them their lives. God's love helped the true virgin Bride to triumph over their fears when it came time to prove their allegiance to the Lord.

I believe I can safely ascertain that prayer was a significant part of their daily lives and helped carry them through this most arduous trial. Fear did not cause them to flee as the others did. Instead, their faith empowered them to take a righteous stand unto death and they were rewarded by God with the gift of life for their obedience and for staying true to their convictions.

You may think, "Oh, I would never deny Jesus!" Peter thought that, too. We don't know what went through the minds of those who left the service in Russia that night. Perhaps one of them had left a wife and newborn child at home; perhaps another was the sole breadwinner for his family; another could have left her children with the neighbors; maybe one of them had ailing parents who depended on him. Who would have taken care of these believers' loved ones if they had been killed for standing up for their faith?

Put yourself in their shoes: would you have been willing to let your children grow up without you? Would you have been willing to risk having them indoctrinated by an atheist government since you wouldn't be there to teach them the truth? Would you have been willing to have your unsaved, alcoholic spouse raise your kids? What if, as a result of your devout faith, everything you owned would be confiscated and every member of your family would be separated—even the children—and put in prison or sent to inhumane, horrifying labor camps? Do you feel a little less certain now about what you would do?

Jesus tells us in Luke 14:26, "If anyone comes to Me and does not hate [love Jesus more than] his father and mother, wife and children, brothers and sisters, yes, and his own life also, he cannot be My disciple." We're used to thinking of idols as being false gods or inanimate objects, but people can be idols, too, if they take the place in our hearts that rightfully belongs to the Lord. If we love anyone, more than we love God, we're saying we don't believe He can take care of them as well as we can.

Then, we'll always be afraid that God might "take us away" from our loved ones. There will always be a root of fear in our hearts which will keep us desperately clinging to them, instead of to Jesus. Who rules your heart? God or fear? Who is your true lover?

THE WISE VIRGIN WILL ENDURE THE HOUR OF TEMPTATION

Only those who are in love with Jesus will endure the hour of temptation. This is why He had encouraged His disciples to pray—so that God, the Father, would empower them to withstand the trial that awaited them when the Lord would be taken from them, arrested and crucified. In Matthew 26:41 He exhorted them, "Watch and pray, lest you enter into temptation. The spirit indeed is willing, but the flesh is weak."

Matthew 26:40-45 records that Jesus found His disciples sleeping not once or twice, but three times! When He was preparing Himself for crucifixion, it was then that He needed the prayerful support of His disciples the most. But they failed Him by giving in to the desires of their flesh rather than using the time to pray for God to strengthen them and their Lord.

Jesus had also prophesied that Peter would deny even knowing Him when the moment of testing arrived. In Mark 14:30 He declared, "Assuredly, I say to you that today, even this night, before the rooster crows twice, you will deny Me three times." Though Peter responded vehemently in verse 31 with, "If I have to die with You, I will not deny You!" as did all the other disciples, Mark 14:72 reveals that Peter wept bitterly because he did indeed "fail the test" as the Lord had prophesied.

Despite our shortcomings, our Groom never sees us as losers, no matter how many times we fail! We just get to take the same test over and over again until we pass, just as Peter finally did in Acts 2:41. He let go of his fear of man because of his love for Jesus and the Holy Spirit filled him with so much boldness and wisdom that he led three thousand people to salvation that day! After that, there was no stopping him. Jesus always gives us the courage to overcome fear, including the fear of death, and this was evident in Peter's life.

I want to emphasize here that when we find ourselves in the same position Peter was in when he folded under pressure, that the Lord will not condemn us, but instead receive us back to Himself through His grace when we repent. Proverbs 24:16 tells us that even though a righteous man or woman may fall seven times, he will not just lay there and wallow in self-pity, but will get back up again, just as Peter did.

God is pleased when we repent because He knows we do so when we realize that we've failed Him and desire to reestablish a holy relationship with Him. Such humility is a sign that we love God because we don't want any sin to stand between us and our Lord. After Christ's resurrection, He restored Peter by allowing him to openly confess his love for Jesus three times before instructing him to be a shepherd for His followers (John 21:15-19).

1 John 4:18-19 declares that, "There is no fear in love; but perfect love casts out [all] fear, because fear involves torment [emphasis author's]. But he who fears has not been made perfect in love." It is the wise virgin who will take the time to love the Lord and not allow any trial or tragedy to stand in the way between her and her Bridegroom.

We must prove ourselves faithful in the area of prayer, lest we weep bitterly as Peter did when he failed the Lord (Mark 14:72). The Lord's true virgin Bride will successfully endure the hour of temptation because she is so in love with Jesus that nothing will distract her from pursuing the One that she loves. She has reservations in Heaven and no one, not even Satan, can prevent her from reaching her destination!

How do I know this? Because 1 John 4:4 makes it unequivocally clear that the Holy Spirit, who lives inside of us, is stronger than Satan in the following passage: "You are of God, little children, and have overcome them, because He who is in you is greater than he who is in the world." Despite temptations that we are constantly surrounded by, the Lord will always empower us to make the right decision at the appointed hour and especially when we are in a crisis. We are also reminded in 1 Corinthians 10:13 that "No temptation has overtaken you except such as is common to man; but God is faithful, who will not allow you to be tempted beyond what you are able, but with the temptation will also make the way of escape, that you may be able to bear it."

This reminds me of a story that Pastor Rich Guerra shared with our congregation about his experiences as a child. He said that it was considered sinful in some denominations to watch a movie at a theater, an extreme belief system that many churches adhered to back then. But he and some of his friends still managed to sneak away and watch a matinee occasionally.

Later, he was asked as a young child by a pastor what he would say if, all of a sudden, the Lord showed up and sat next to him at a cinema. After a few moments of thinking about this, he said, "That's easy. I would say, 'Would you like some popcorn, Jesus?'" What a precious answer from the pure heart of a beautiful child!

This young boy had nothing to hide because he went to see a movie with pure motives and was even prepared to offer His Savior a snack in the event that He decided to join him. I pray that the Lord will help all of us as the Bride of Christ to be faithful to Him until we reach our destination— the theater or Heaven—whatever comes first!

ARE YOU GETTING READY?

When a young woman gets ready for a date with her fiancé, she can literally spend hours preparing: showering, styling her hair, choosing the right clothes, applying make-up, and this doesn't even include all the time spent anticipating and daydreaming about her future husband's arrival! If Jesus were to return today, would He find you ready? Would you be holy and acceptable in His sight or would He find you contaminated by the evil in this world, culminating in your walk with Him being overridden with fear?

What are you doing to get ready for Christ's return? Are you committed to loving your husband, wife, girlfriend, boyfriend or fiancé and others through the life of integrity that you live? If you have not already begun to do so, it's time to get your spiritual house in order. God is preparing an eternal home for His glorious church—for those who have kept themselves pure from immorality. If you truly belong to Jesus, you'll give Him permission to sweep away every childish habit which you've allowed to take root and produce fear in your life so His love can perfect you.

Trust God to prepare you for that joyful day of the Marriage Supper of the Lamb when we'll be forever united with our most wonderful, amazing Jesus, whose ardent love for us will never be quenched! Listen to the promise that God gives us as He prepares us for that eventful time in Revelation 19:5-9:

> Then a voice came from the throne, saying, "Praise our God, all you His servants and those who fear Him, both small and great!"
>
> And I heard, as it were, the voice of a great multitude, as the sound of many waters and as the sound of mighty thunderings, saying, "Alleluia! For the Lord God Omnipotent reigns! Let us be glad and rejoice and give Him glory, for the marriage of the Lamb has come, and His wife has made herself ready." And to her it was granted to be arrayed in fine linen, clean and bright, for the fine linen is the righteous acts of the saints.
>
> Then he said to me, "Write: 'Blessed are those who are called to the marriage supper of the Lamb!'" And he said to me, "These are the true sayings of God."

It is indeed the mature Christian who can honestly look inside himself and realize there will always be a part of him that will be unfulfilled until he goes to be with the Lord. According to Dr. Larry Crabb, Christian counselor and author of *Inside Out*, "When we look carefully at what we deeply desire, we come to realize that what we want is simply not available, not until Heaven. The more aware we become of our most passionate longings, the more lonely and sad we feel." [9]

The complete joys of God will not be ours until Paradise. There will always be a deep ache and longing that nothing and no one on this side of Heaven can ever fill—not Christian retreats or seminars, revival meetings or intense prayer and study of the Word, not challenging projects in the mission fields, or even our spouse or romantic partner. All of these wholesome influences are good because they strengthen us spiritually and God desires that we partake of them. But the empty aching we feel is like the deep, intense longing that two lovers experience when they must be apart; we are the Bride of Christ and we desperately yearn for the Wedding Day! Come quickly, Lord Jesus!

THE BRIDE OF CHRIST

As you prepare for Jesus Christ's return
Will He still find you faithful as you place your hope in Him?
Knowing salvation is a gift that can't be earned
Will your light still be shining or go faintly dim!

Keep in mind, dear one, that your faith may soon be tested.
Many saints will be beaten and others put to death,
Some brutally tortured, while others are arrested.
Will you still preach the Good News until your dying breath?

The Church of God is ailing and bound with deadly fear.
Heartache and disappointment have snatched its joy away.
We've forgotten that Jesus is always very near,
And that the Holy Spirit forever guides us when we pray.

He will soon be returning for a glorious Bride
That has kept herself pure, despite the evil of the day.
Will He find you dressed in white or will you run and hide
When He declares: "Come, all who've listened and obeyed!"

Will you be wise or foolish when the Son of God returns?
Is your heart's lamp filled with oil and steadily burning,
Or is it empty, darkened, frozen and preserved?
A fearful way of life is not what God is yearning.

Are you at peace in knowing that God is pleased with your walk,
Or are you dreadfully worried that you've let the Lord down?
Have you walked the Christian way or simply talked the talk?
For the true worshipers will inherit their Heavenly crowns.

True believers are excited that Jesus is alive!
They shout with triumph, dance with joy, and live in victory.
They are led by God's Spirit and have learned how to thrive
Because they know that His faithfulness is part of history.

"The hour has arrived for My church to repent,
For I will bless My own with its Heavenly reward.
Don't forget that Jesus, My Son, was mercifully sent.
Seek the way of redemption, My child, and be restored.

"I'm preparing My Church for the Marriage Supper of the
   Lamb.
Do not go the way of destruction, which is far and wide.
But follow My leading, for I am the great 'I AM.'
You are the Bride of Christ for whom I joyfully died."

CHAPTER THREE

A CRITICAL VERSUS A LOVING SPIRIT

"...no man can tame the tongue. It is an unruly evil, full of
deadly poison. With it we bless our God and Father, and with
it we curse men, who have been made in the similitude of God.
Out of the same mouth proceed blessing and cursing.
My brethren, these things ought not to be so."
(James 3:8-10)

As we continue on our journey of falling in love with
Jesus, we must be honest about areas in our lives that are not
pleasing to Him. Those of us who come from an abusive or
neglectful environment frequently end up badly beaten and
bruised emotionally by those who should have loved us the
most. This kind of pain is one of the most difficult for us to
face; the anguish of realizing the depth of the emotional
betrayal involved often seems like too much to bear.

Afraid of facing this deep heartache, we choose to
withdraw from close relationships (even with God) and we
revile (verbally abuse) others before we can be hurt again
ourselves. Instead of facing our sorrows, we habitually displace
our hurt and anger on the innocent because we're ignorant of
how to channel our emotional wounds appropriately. Many
times, we aren't even aware that we're inflicting pain on others
but realize we need to get the heartache out somehow in order to
survive.

However, humiliating people does not ease our suffering.
Instead, it worsens our situation because it is the opposite of
what we're commanded to do in Leviticus 19:18, Matthew
5:43-45 and Romans 13:9: "You shall love your neighbor as
yourself."

When a banana is left too long in the fruit bowl, it spoils.
Likewise, when the pain of past hurts and unforgiveness are kept
too long in our hearts, rottenness sets in and it affects everything
we do. Being judgmental is the product of an unforgiving heart,
as Jesus so clearly points out in Luke 6:45, "A good man out of
the good treasure of his heart brings forth good; and an evil man

out of the evil treasure of his heart brings forth evil. For out of the abundance of the heart his mouth speaks."

We may be able to hide this defilement for years, but, eventually, the sin that we have so carefully and conveniently concealed will infuse every thought, word and deed, just as the smell of a decaying banana can permeate a room. It may be out of sight, but everyone will know it's there.

THE SIN OF REVILING

John and Daisy had been a "happily" married, Christian couple for six years. However, in the course of having four babies in close succession, paying the monthly bills and dealing with the stresses of everyday life, the children had become the focus of their marriage. Since the romantic overtures of their courtship had long since vanished, Daisy felt neglected as a woman, unloved and rejected by her husband.

She didn't like confrontation, so she ignored her anger toward John. Soon, the sweet spirit which first drew him to Daisy disappeared, and in its place, a critical spirit took root in the bitterness of her heart. Because she secretly blamed her children for stealing her husband's time as well as her youthfulness and joy, she began to verbally abuse them by lashing out in rage at the smallest provocation.

At first, she was horrified at her outbursts and immediately asked her children to forgive her. For a while, that seemed to work while she hid this from John. But soon, her tirades spilled over into the evenings and were directed toward her husband. Because she was unwilling and afraid to face her wounded soul, over time, she began making disparaging remarks to her friends.

Whenever this would happen, she would be deeply embarrassed and attempted to cover up her attacks by minimizing, "Please forgive me. I've been under a lot of stress lately. That was not the real me."

This reminds me of a story that a pastor once shared with his congregation when he was talking about the gift of self-control. He commented that Christian husbands and wives sometimes let their emotions get out of control as evidenced when they communicate disrespectfully.

He went on to say, "How many of you know if I were to visit you unexpectedly and knock on your door right when you're in the middle of an argument that you would immediately shift in a second's time to a peaceful state, smile, and say, 'Oh, Hi, Pastor John!'" In other words, your negative attitude would be instantly gone because you chose to exercise self-control and crucify your fleshly desires.

People with a critical spirit may not be aware at that moment that they could practice self-control with a little bit of effort. Granted, they may not know the source of their anger because they're so accustomed to belittling others rather than asking God to help them identify the root of their hurt. They may be too <u>afraid</u> to face their pain. However, it's a selfish, inexcusable way for Christians to live and is not an accurate representation of the true Bride of Christ, who is committed to facing anything ungodly within her that would endanger her witness for the Lord.

The world is plagued with people who malign others, but in the Christian realm, there is no place for believers to continue to exist in those childish ways, especially since we're no longer children. Our hurts need to be laid at God's altar before our suppressed emotions cause us and others to falter. Jesus told the Pharisees, "You are those who justify yourselves [rationalize] before men, but God knows your hearts. For what is highly esteemed among men is an abomination in the sight of God" (Luke 16:15).

We are not Pharisees, which means we should not act like them! We are the Bride of Christ. This means that before we reek with bitterness outside of our home, the Lord will, first, gently expose our shortcomings so we can seek Him for healing and restoration because of His amazing love and gracious mercy. He constantly gives us an opportunity to work out the wounds that pierce our souls in a private setting. That's His favor and we should always answer His call for repentance.

Be aware, however, that if Jesus is truly our Lord and Savior, yet we stubbornly refuse to heed His warnings for us to change and continue to rationalize our sins, He'll be left with no other option but to chasten us by publicly exposing our flaws to get us to repent. It's like an infection—the longer it sits uncared for, the more visible it becomes and the more the body is infected and, in this case, one's physical body as well as the Body of Christ. God's grace is manifested as He makes our open wound more obvious until we can see it clearly enough to deal with it in a mature manner.

Unfortunately, after God gave Daisy numerous opportunities to face her pain, to repent privately and allow the Lord to embrace her with His healing love, she rejected every loving option that He gave her. Soon, after a few weeks of her public explosions, her friends stopped calling her and John withdrew from her even more. Our actions speak louder than our words, and when we continue to insist that our dark side is not really us, our actions cry out, "That was the real you! Who else would it be? Why do you think your friends don't call you anymore?"

Once we realize that our loved ones have distanced themselves because they don't want anything to do with our negative attitude, the light comes on. This is, hopefully, when we'll allow God to convince us to hand over our pain to Him so He can heal us from within while we surrender our sin. And once our friends and loved ones see our new attitude, they'll come out of their hiding places because they'll see us acting civilized again. We all have a dark side; we just need to remember to crucify it as soon as it manifests itself, especially since it affects those who love us the most.

In the loneliness caused by her self-imposed exile, Daisy was convicted of defying God's clear command to forgive her husband and of refusing to take responsibility for her own actions. Please realize that God takes no delight in humbling His children! He would much rather speak to us privately, as a Father to His wayward son or daughter. The Lord still poured out His love to Daisy; He just had to do it after she realized she was all alone for a reason—because she was still trying to deal with her hurt by reverting to her childish ways—by displacing her wounds on the innocent rather than facing her pain as a responsible believer.

God will not allow us to infect the Body of Christ (His beloved Bride) without reproving us in some way. If we fail to humble ourselves before the Lord privately, He will humble us publicly. Jesus tells us in Luke 12:2-3, "For there is nothing covered that will not be revealed, nor hidden that will not be known. Therefore whatever you have spoken in the dark will be heard in the light, and what you have spoken in the ear in inner rooms will be proclaimed on the housetops." God loves us just the same in both the public and private arenas but He prefers to get our attention as soon as possible because He doesn't like to see us suffer more than we have to.

This reminds me of when I was in my sophomore year in college. I became friends with Robert Nguyen, a friendly, genuine college roommate who was very gifted socially and cared a great deal about people. He invested much of his time in building relationships, which is why he was so popular.

After he had established a good, strong friendship with me, he noticed I never apologized when the situation called for it and that I was quick to blame others or circumstances when things didn't go my way. One day, he approached me and posed this question: "Victor—have you ever noticed that you never apologize when you make a mistake?" He immediately grabbed my attention. I responded, "No, Robert; I haven't."

As we talked further, he helped me to take a long, hard look at my childhood. He ascertained that my dad was very judgmental, prideful, rarely apologized to anyone and typically lashed out in anger when he had a problem with someone. I was an easy scapegoat and helpless victim as he ridiculed me when I failed to hold a shovel properly, couldn't remember his instructions or get high enough grades to please him. Robert helped me to realize that I had taken on this negative attitude besides embracing a victim mentality.

Granted, our parents aren't perfect and it isn't fair when they snap at us viciously in their feeble attempt to discipline us when they're out of control. They have character flaws like anyone else but it doesn't really help us to change by blaming our shortcomings on them. This heart-to-heart talk with Robert helped me because it was one of the first times that I seriously looked at how I could make peace with issues related to my childhood.

Over time, the Holy Spirit showed me that at the root of my failure to apologize was emotional pain, deep-seated anger and feeling mistreated as a child by my dad. The Lord helped me to face these hurts in my mid-twenties and again in my early thirties. He built badly-needed humility in me that was sorely lacking and, today, I have no problem asking for forgiveness when I fall short in communicating.

A critical (judgmental) spirit had been passed on to me, but I realized that, as a young adult, it was up to me to shoulder responsibility for my actions. I quickly learned that we are all a "work in progress." This will never change until we go to be with the Lord in Heaven one day.

ARE YOU A MODERN DAY PHARISEE OR A TRUE CHRISTIAN?

Author Dick Eastman believes that our nation's number one sin is criticism [a judgmental spirit] and that it creates an ineffectual prayer life because of its roots of bitterness and hatred that get in the way.[10] He states, "Nothing gives Satan a free hand—destroying efforts of bended knees—more than the spirit of criticism. Of all the weapons in Satan's arsenal, this one most assuredly is the greatest. In truth, what prayer means to God, criticism means to Satan." [11] Prayer is the key that unlocks healing in your life. It conveys to God that you're serious about being healed as you continue to seek Him while believing that He'll heal your desolate places—your broken and lonely heart.

Unfortunately, people who degrade others are typically not people who pray with pure motives, nor are they interested in listening to God. If they were, the Holy Spirit would have convicted them by now and they would have received His insight, direction, and a plan of healing for their lives. Their prayers are filled with complaints and criticisms to the Lord. These people do the majority of the talking while they expect God to do most of the listening.

Their prayers are rooted in false pride rather than humility since they don't approach God's throne-room with the expressed purpose of allowing Christ to change them. Instead, their prayers are intended to manipulate God so they can get their own way. James 4:3 describes them as not receiving answers to their prayers because they pray amiss with a selfish agenda.

The Pharisees are classic examples of religious people who suffered from a critical spirit. As adept as they were in living according to the letter of the law, the traditions of the elders and in presenting a holy appearance, externally-speaking, they were miserable people who hindered many others who desired to know the True and Living God. When Jesus addressed the multitudes when he preached a sermon on "The Beatitudes," He declared, "unless your righteousness exceeds the righteousness of the scribes and Pharisees, you will by no means enter the kingdom of heaven" (Matthew 5:20). I can't help but wonder if some of his audience might have pondered, "If the Pharisees can't live righteously and make it to Heaven, then what chance do we have?"

A key lesson here is that we cannot rely on our own ability to fulfill the law to live a righteous life; we must rely on God's ability (Matthew 5:17). Perhaps Walt Kelly (1913-1973), an American animator and cartoonist, captured this point best. He popularized a central character named Pogo through a daily comic strip distributed by the Post-Hall Syndicate. As he was trying to make a point on environmental safety on Earth Day in 1970, he coined the phrase, "We have met the enemy and he is us." [12]

Our sinful nature continuously stares at us in the mirror and we see our reflection each time we fail over and over again. Romans 3:23 soberly reminds us that we'll never reach moral perfection here on earth "for all have sinned and fall short of the glory of God."

In Matthew 15:3-6, Jesus confronted the scribes and Pharisees about the evil intent of their hearts. He reminded them that they had failed to live by the same standards that they expected common people to follow and He accused them of rationalizing their sins through their useless traditions. In verses 7-9, He drove His point even further when He nailed them to a cross: "Hypocrites! Well did Isaiah prophesy about you saying: 'These people draw near to Me with their mouth, and honor Me with their lips, but their heart is far from Me. And in vain they worship Me, teaching as doctrines the commandments of men.'" Jesus was fed up with their double standards and exposed these religious leaders for what they really were—wolves in sheep's clothing.

Though the Pharisees were elaborately dressed, culturally refined, verbally sophisticated, and socially accepted as intellectual and religious giants, their hearts were just as dark and sinful as the Gentiles they despised. They were spiritually lost themselves, despite claiming to know the Lord, because they esteemed the customs of men more than the commandments of God. Jesus describes how He felt about their sinful natures in the following passages:

> Woe to you, scribes and Pharisees, hypocrites!
> For you cleanse the outside of the cup and
> dish, but inside they are full of extortion and
> self-indulgence. Blind Pharisee, first cleanse
> the inside of the cup and dish, that the outside
> of them may be clean also.
>
> Woe to you, scribes and Pharisees, hypocrites!
> For you are like whitewashed tombs which
> indeed appear beautiful outwardly, but
> inside are full of dead men's bones and all
> uncleanness. Even so you also outwardly
> appear righteous to men, but inside you are
> full of hypocrisy and lawlessness
> (Matthew 23:25-28).

The Pharisees' critical spirit was easily seen as they attacked Jesus time and time again, especially after He performed miracles of healing. They accused Him of sinning for curing a blind man on the Sabbath (John 9:6-7,14,16). They also sought to kill Him for healing a lame man on the Sabbath and for claiming equality with God when He said the Lord was His Father (John 5:5-18). They belittled Him for eating with sinners (Matthew 9:10-11) and ridiculed Him when He cured a paralytic because He boldly declared that the man's sins were forgiven (Luke 5:17-26).

Furthermore, these religious leaders harassed Jesus' disciples for not obeying the tradition of the elders of ceremoniously washing their hands before eating bread (Mark 7:5). These are examples of religious people who were so bound by worthless tradition that when the Savior of the world finally came to visit them and offer them redemption, they sought to destroy Him because upholding man-made laws was more important to them than their own salvation or the salvation of others.

A perfectionist is a modern-day example of a Pharisee. He believes in upholding the letter of the law. This is not to say the Ten Commandments, but the law that he has created in his own mind as an addendum. This brings to mind a hilarious movie, *History of the World: Part 1*. As the Old Testament is reenacted, one scene shows Moses, played by Mel Brooks, coming down from Mount Sinai and holding three stone tablets.

Then, he announces to the Israelites, "The Lord Jehova has given unto you these fifteen—"[Smash!]"… [Make that] Ten—Ten Commandments for all to obey!" [13] As perfectionistic as the Pharisees were, I would not have been surprised if they would have insisted on replacing the so-called missing tablet with their own set of rules.

Fortunately, Mel Brooks saves the day in this fictional, yet comical scene by attempting to convey that not only is God merciful by just requiring us to obey these ten golden standards, but that He has a sense of humor! Some of us may even be thinking, "Thank God that it was only ten and not fifteen commandments that we need to follow!"

Since he's afraid to face his own pain, the perfectionist does everything humanly possible to live as if he's in control to shield himself from further hurt in his life. As we said earlier, these "walls" merely contribute to his ongoing pain. He cannot stand imperfection in others because it reminds him of his own shortcomings.

Of course, the modern-day Pharisee doesn't wear long robes, but is easily recognized by the trail of devastation he leaves behind. He lives to find fault in those around him and becomes easily irritated, especially with co-workers and family members, when they're not able to meet his unrealistic expectations. He may even blame his angry disposition on his ancestry by saying he blows up occasionally because of his Irish, Samoan, or German temper or claim that he's just a moody person.

Don't be deceived! Blaming is no excuse for not

trusting God to do a badly-needed character change within us. The Lord doesn't lower His standards for us just because of our ancestral roots or because we have a certain temperament. For us to use our personality type as an excuse for not living up to the moral principles that God has given us is, in reality, <u>rationalizing</u> the sin of pride.

Many of us lived this type of lifestyle before our conversion to Christ. However, it's indeed a tragedy when we call ourselves Christians, yet still operate out of this childish mentality because it means that total surrender to Christ has not truly happened. In reality, people who function this way are Christians by name only; they thrive on living in the limelight exactly as the Pharisees did, but inside, they are just as full of death as a whitewashed tomb (Matthew 23:27). If this uncleanness pervades their hearts, sooner or later, it <u>will</u> be made known publicly.

I used to attend a church whose pastor was well-known and respected both in Christian circles and in the community at large. However, he regularly made fun of his wife from the pulpit. When people would tell him that it bothered them when he made his spouse the brunt of a joke, he'd simply shrug and say, "You know I'm only joking, don't you?" He was <u>rationalizing</u> and <u>minimizing</u> his sin in addition to being insensitive to how his transgression was affecting the members of this congregation.

Unfortunately, this sort of criticism is infectious. Soon, the youth pastor began to ridicule his assistant and the music director was overheard using racial slurs to identify one of the musicians. Even though there are many reputable, devout church leaders, these poor examples are often the ones the media showcases unmercifully so the world can label them as "hypocrites," thus keeping unbelievers from the faith and poisoning the minds of devout followers in houses of worship.

Is this the example of love that we should be showing the world? Of course not! We'll never know how many Christian men and teenage boys now think it's perfectly acceptable to bully their wives or girlfriends in public or how many people now excuse their own prejudice because of the bad examples presented by these insensitive spiritual leaders.

We should never victimize anyone through a tasteless joke—we should always keep our humor clean. We need to repent and consecrate ourselves daily so God can bless us as we come before Him with a pure heart. Exodus 32:29 reminds us about the importance of this concept, "Consecrate yourselves today to the Lord, that He may bestow on you a blessing this day…"

God expects us to live by high moral values and to assume responsibility for the high calling that He's placed upon us as the Bride of Christ. We need to act like believers, lest we be exposed as a fraud in the same manner in which Jesus exposed the religious leaders of his day as hypocrites. <u>Let's not forget that we are Christians, not Pharisees, because Jesus has not only saved us from the enemy of our souls but He has saved us from ourselves</u>!

A CRITICAL SPIRIT IS THE #1 THREAT TO CHRISTIAN MARRIAGES

Emotionally-speaking, I have found that a critical spirit is not only the foremost threat to the institution of marriage, but to relationships as well. Selfishness and false pride form the core roots of an abusive tongue that seeks to destroy what God has put together. This negative spirit does not know mercy, understanding, love or compassion. This description can only fit one character: Satan. The enemy has always been busy working to see who he can influence to do his dirty work for him.

Though divorce has infiltrated the Christian Church, contrary to popular belief, "…the divorce rate among Christians is significantly lower than the general population…Couples who regularly…attend church nearly every week, read their Bibles…pray privately and together, generally take their faith seriously…enjoy significantly lower divorce rates than mere church members, the general public and unbelievers." [14] Also, in a study conducted by Professor Bradley Wright, a sociologist at the University of Connecticut, he discovered that only 38% of those who identify themselves as Christians and attend church regularly have been divorced." [15]

This empirical evidence supports the belief that married people who consistently practice their religious faith experience the blessings of staying together. God helps Christian married couples who seek Him for help. Psalm 145:18 reminds us that "The Lord is near to all who call upon Him, to all who call upon Him in truth."

Sad to say, many believers fall prey to Satan's deadly devices rather than pay heed to God's holy commandment in Exodus 20:16, which states, "You shall not bear false witness against your neighbor." Christian married couples especially need to take this commandment very seriously if they want their marriage to be divorce-proof. Your "neighbor" includes your marriage partner! Galatians 5:14-15 further illustrates the significance of love and mutual respect, "For all the law is fulfilled in one word, even in this: 'You shall love your neighbor as yourself.' But if you bite and devour one another, beware lest you be consumed by one another!"

This reminds me of a story I once heard of a man who was seeking counsel from a mature, upstanding citizen from his local community. When he asked this gentleman what his perception was of him, he was slow to comment, paused some more, crossed his arms and thought for a moment. As he continued to ponder, the man who asked the question grew impatient and said, "Well, do you have anything to tell me?"

The gentleman contemplated deeply, paused again and responded with, "Bill, in all honesty, I have to say that you come across as a selfish person." Surprised, Bill replied, "Do you mind if I get a second opinion?" This gentleman replied, "Certainly. And you're ugly, too!" Somehow, I don't think this is what Bill had in mind! He felt disrespected and rightfully so.

Men, here's an especially urgent message for you: <u>if you do not treat your wives with respect</u>, 1 Peter 3:7 says that <u>God will not hear your prayers</u>. He continues in verses 8-12 to confront couples with these words:

> Finally, all of you be of one mind, having compassion for one another; love as brothers, be tenderhearted, be courteous; not returning evil for evil or reviling for reviling, but on

the contrary blessing, knowing that you were called to this [in your marriage] that you may inherit a blessing.

For "He who would love life and see good days, let him refrain his tongue from evil, and his lips from speaking deceit; Let him turn away from evil and do good; let him seek peace and pursue it. For the eyes of the Lord are on the righteous, And His ears are open to their prayers; But the face of the Lord is against those who do evil."

Verbal abuse is evil. James even describes the tongue of those who are led by the flesh as being "set on fire by hell," which is a very graphic illustration and shows how serious God is about controlling what comes out of our mouths (James 3:6). But how many of us truly realize that all those little, cutting remarks, the murmuring, the fault-finding and the criticizing that we so easily give in to daily are causing the Lord to turn His face <u>against</u> us?

Couples who claim to be Christians and who continually abuse each other verbally (or in any other way) are deceiving themselves; they are rebelling against God. And whenever blatant sin and disregard for the Lord's guidelines are present in someone's life, demonic forces will not be long in coming to take that person hostage. James 4:7 says, "...submit to God. Resist the devil and he will flee from you."

Therefore, if you're not willing to submit every part of yourself as a living sacrifice to God, Satan doesn't have to flee! In fact, he'll come in like a flood to wreak terror. The enemy is relentless in attacking you until he finds an area that is not surrendered to the Lord.

He's like a tenacious, grueling running back—he plows through a defense as if it wasn't even there with the mindset that no one can stop him. So, the sooner you plug those holes that have ushered in compromise and replace them with accountability partners who are clothed with honesty and integrity, the stronger your foundation will be and the tougher it will be for your foe to penetrate your defensive linemen—your spiritual stronghold. Psalm 18:2 declares, "...you [Lord] are my rock and my fortress." Proverbs 18:10 also proclaims that "The name of the Lord is a strong tower; the righteous run to it and are safe."

I once counseled a couple who refused to listen to just about anything I suggested to them. Elliot and Jenny had both been hurt badly by other dating partners in the past, but they still insisted on getting married before working through their previous hurts. Despite my solemn recommendation that they wait until they could become more emotionally stable, they rejected my counsel.

They stopped coming to counseling for a while, but as the fighting between them escalated, they literally described seeing a dark presence in their home one day during the heat of an argument. At that point, they stopped arguing and tried counseling again. Unfortunately, our sessions were filled with their tirades over what indignity each had committed against the other as they dragged up the same garbage over and over again. Since they chose to give in to their fleshly desires—they failed to show each other the courtesy of listening while the other spoke.

When I asked them point-blank if they were willing to work to save their marriage and if they were committed to doing whatever God's Word told them to do, they hesitated and could not give me a definitive answer, even though they both claimed to be Christians! We discussed all the scriptures that we've covered here and more, but they were still not willing to submit to God and to forgive each other. Shortly thereafter, I stopped seeing them because they weren't committed to allowing God to heal them. They were afraid to trust Him with their deepest hurts.

Sometimes, I wonder what it will take to open the eyes of rebellious people to the error of their ways. The experience Elliot and Jenny described would have been more than enough to cause me to repent. I wish I could say that every couple that I counsel is able to change for the better, but ultimately, everyone must decide for themselves whether or not to submit to the Lord.

If you have a spouse who is abusive, God will not accept "he did it first" as a reason to excuse your own critical spirit. Thankfully, I've seen some marriages saved because one partner deliberately chose to bridle his or her tongue. Isaiah 53:7 illustrates to us that it is the silent witness of Jesus in that one's life ("He was oppressed and He was afflicted, yet He opened not His mouth") that enables the abuser to be convicted of his sin. I'm not saying that you should allow the abuse to continue, especially if children are involved, but only that <u>no one has the right to verbally abuse or humiliate anyone, for we are all made in the image of God</u>. Often in silence, the observer sees qualities such as humility, love, joy, peace, patience, and perseverance at work in the believer's life, which brings conviction on the unbeliever.

To clarify, I'm not advocating here that the silent witness be a doormat for her abusive husband. Please don't misunderstand me. Sometimes the abused victim needs to lovingly confront her spouse and demand change so he doesn't get away with a bad attitude and see it turn into a huge mountain over time. She needs to be able to paint a vivid picture and speak in her spouse's love language so he clearly understands how much he's hurting her.

It may even be necessary for that abused spouse to give her partner an ultimatum, "You have six months to get your life in order or I'm leaving you" with the hope that he's listening intently. And if he doesn't change, then perhaps during the separation time, reality will set in and he'll hopefully come to terms with the darkness of his sin, with how much of a goldmine his wife really is, and realize that he needs to treat her like the lovely princess that he once treasured and courted.

To choose to do nothing, however, and hope that your wayward husband will effectuate changes on his own is not a viable choice. Why? It isn't realistic. He needs to feel pressure to change. Otherwise, he's not likely to take any action. This is called tough love and it's a much better option than dissolution.

When another couple, Bob and Elizabeth, came to see me, they were also on the brink of filing for a divorce. Elizabeth told me that Bob constantly criticized her about everything she did. He told her the clothes she wore made her look fat, he didn't like how she wore her hair, she had too much make-up on, she didn't have enough make-up on, she couldn't cook a decent meal, he didn't like her friends, and on and on the abuse and controlling behavior went.

Their daughter also couldn't do anything right in his eyes, and, even though she was only in third grade, Bob reprimanded her daily for not doing better in school and sports. As Elizabeth poured out their story with much tears and sorrow, Bob would often interrupt her with rationalizations of why he was right. Even so, she refused to take the bait to get into an argument with him.

Proverbs 10:11 declares, "The mouth of the righteous is a well of life, but <u>violence covers the mouth of the</u> <u>wicked</u>" [emphasis author's]. A critical tongue leaves a trail of innocent blood in that we can't help but affect those around us by the way we terrorize them with our vicious mouths. The Holy Bible clearly states that there will be a very heavy price to pay, eternally-speaking, for anyone who harms His precious children.

In 1 Corinthians 6:9-10, the Apostle Paul talks about the judgment of God. When he addresses <u>revilers</u> (those who criticize or commit murder with their mouths), he is clear about disclosing the penalty for this sin—eternal punishment. Moreover, In 1 Corinthians 5:11, he warns us that we are not to associate with a brother or sister in Christ who is immoral so that we should not become like them.

After Elizabeth had finished speaking, I asked Bob what his home life had been like when he was a child. He graphically described having been ridiculed for everything he did wrong. His dad mocked him for not mowing the lawn properly, not getting high enough grades (despite making the honor roll list consistently), and not hustling enough in baseball. Through this cruel upbringing, Bob had learned to see his Heavenly Father as harsh, demanding, and judgmental.

As a result, Bob learned how to bully other people, manipulate circumstances, expect perfection from others and ridicule anyone who didn't meet his impossible standards. The resulting load of guilt that he had carried through the years was overwhelming and each time the Lord had tried to break through to his aching heart, Bob had shut Him out, afraid of being hurt even more.

However, each time we attempt to postpone a work that God is doing in our lives, He'll set us up to experience the same life lessons over and over again until we allow Him to be in control and complete the task at hand. Philippians 1:6 states,

"He who has begun a good work in you <u>will</u> complete it until the day of Jesus Christ…" [emphasis author's]. If we continue to wrestle with God for control of our lives, we'll have nothing to turn to but our fleshly, ineffective survival mechanisms.

As Bob realized that he'd been raised by an unhealthy, bitter father, he began to understand where his own critical nature came from. As he became willing to face his hurt and anger, he was able to ask his wife and child to forgive him for his abusive ways, and was able to renounce the false guilt that he had carried for so long. When Bob learned how to trust God with his heart issues, he discovered that he no longer had a reason to hurt people, to control his home and work environment, or to blame the Lord for the trials he had to endure.

God's love penetrated through his critical self. In this situation, had his wife "stood up for her rights" and harshly criticized him in return, he might not have been convicted of his own sin because love is absent when a judgmental spirit dominates a conversation. Contrast the marriage of Elliot and Jenny with that of Bob and Elizabeth: Bob was "won by the conduct" of his wife (1 Peter 3:1), since the Lord was able to convict him of senseless pain that he was inflicting on his wife and daughter.

On the other hand, when I last checked with Elliot and Jenny, they were still miserable because they refused to put their partner's interests above their own. Their marriage can be summed up with this phrase from James 3:16, "For where envy and self-seeking exist, confusion and every evil thing are there."

A LOOK IN THE MIRROR

It might seem easy at this point to say, "Well, I'm glad I'm not like that!" But how often have we criticized God? How often have we been quick to murmur and complain during the pruning of our characters and the testing of our faith? Since we, in this generation, are accustomed to this world's fast-paced life, we also expect God to act in a similar fashion. When the Lord does not provide an answer according to our timelines, it's easy to grow more impatient and judgmental, both of Him and of the unfortunate people who happen to be around us at that time.

While our Heavenly Father attempts to build our faith and strengthen and shape our characters, how many of us instead continue to battle with God for control by attempting to manipulate circumstances to the point where we believe that we've gained an advantage? Each time the Lord turns up the heat, does the verbal artillery start to fly? When we attempt to sabotage God's plans for the purifying and strengthening of our faith, is it because we're afraid of giving up control of our lives to Him?

Can you imagine how ridiculous we must look when we waver in our faith in the Lord? We may say "I trust You, Father" with our words in one moment and "I don't trust You" with our actions a few minutes later. Yet, letting go of control is the very thing that someone who abuses others needs the most! When it comes right down to it, negative people don't really believe deep in their hearts that God desires to bless them or that what they do on Sunday should have any impact on how they live the other six days of the week.

Here's a quick self-test to see whether you fall in this category:

- When the checker at the grocery store moves at a snail's pace, do you grumble and murmur to yourself or to others in line?
- Do you act pleasantly when a policeman pulls you over for speeding, then complain about it afterwards, or even speak badly about his character for upholding the law?
- When someone maneuvers his car to take the parking space that you've been waiting for, do profane words come unbidden from your tongue?
- Have you ever ridiculed your child or spouse by asking them, "How could you have been so stupid? What on earth were you thinking?"
- Have you ever shared private information with someone about another person when you knew it should have been kept confidential? Afterwards, did you use the excuse that you wanted to "share" so others would know how to pray in rationalizing your sinful behavior?

If you still struggle in some of these areas, be aware of what issues God still needs to work on you to build more peace, joy and love into your heart. We all struggle in bridling our tongues at some point in time. But if you find you cannot control what comes out of your mouth, then it could be that you are in bondage. James 1:26 states quite clearly, "If anyone among you thinks he is religious, and does not bridle his tongue but deceives his own heart, this one's religion is useless."

FINDING EMOTIONAL AND SPIRITUAL FREEDOM

Such a monster can only be tamed through the Holy Spirit Himself. Only He can bring self-control to those of us who lack the heavenly wisdom of when and how to keep our mouths shut. With this in mind, I've been asked at times how I keep clients' issues confidential. My response is, "That's easy. I literally get paid to keep my mouth shut!" They often laugh when I say this, but it's the truth.

If you've previously trusted Christ as your Savior, you can trust Him as your Healer but you must choose to give Him permission to examine the source of your critical spirit and prescribe a cure. Are you willing? Regardless of what your circumstances are, God will help you overcome your abusive tongue as well as all the other mind-games that hold you captive, if you'll allow Him to.

God wants to transform our spirits into those which bless and love others through our words and actions. Let's look at three areas which are lacking in the life of someone who verbally abuses others but must be present in the lives of those who wish to be set free. They include: 1) an ability to forgive others, 2) a repentant heart that has chosen to die of its old, sinful ways, and 3) a desire to exercise self-control.

FORGIVING OTHERS

Those who habitually criticize others frequently have unresolved bitterness and anger toward people who abused them. Every person I've met with in counseling desired to be freed of this stronghold, but not all were willing to do what was required of them—to forgive those who offended, neglected or betrayed them. Those who chose to not forgive others continued to carry the poison of abuse, betrayal and isolation from previous relationships where a loved one failed to meet their emotional needs and purposely hurt them. These wounded victims were able to painstakingly recall the specifics of their hurt week after week, but when it came time to forgive their perpetrators, their responses included, "Never," "Not now," "I'm not ready to do that," or "Only if he asks me to forgive him first!"

They rationalized why they had every right to not forgive the person who inflicted pain on them. They felt that no one had ever gone through the same amount of suffering they had experienced. Even the biblical precept that if they do not forgive others, Christ cannot forgive them (which means they cannot enter Heaven) did not change their minds!

Forgiving others is not a feeling, but a choice, and, according to Pastor Paul Goulet (author of the *Reconcilers* series), forgiveness does not normally happen instantaneously, but takes time. [16] In this culture of fast food, quick tellers, rapid transit and instant coffee, we're not accustomed to waiting and often feel irritated when we depend on others to cater to us. As Christians, we are the ones who must wait on God, not the other way around.

Jesus said in Matthew 18:22 that we must be willing to forgive those who hurt us "not up to seven times, but up to seventy times seven." He did not mean that we can literally count four hundred and ninety times and then say, "That's it! I don't have to forgive you anymore!" Rather, Jesus was showing us that we need to be willing to forgive someone an infinite amount of times. Forgiveness is a choice—that's the first act of obedience.

Next, the process is where we must continuously forgive for as long as we're working through hurt, anger, rejection and betrayal. When there is no more pain associated with the memory of the hurtful event, we'll know we have reached the state of forgiveness. [17] It may take some longer to reach this destination than others, depending on how deep one's wounds are, but we know God is faithful to complete the healing work that He began (Philippians 1:6).

The resulting change in the hearts of those who were willing to let go of their hurts and unforgiving mindset was truly beautiful to see. Though some were reluctant to forgive at first, those who forgave were healed through the power of the Holy Spirit. They realized that in order to obey their Heavenly Father, forgiving others was not a choice, but a commandment they had to submit to. They knew they wouldn't be able to forgive others on their own—but through God's strength, they succeeded in doing so.

Tony had battled depression for years; it was difficult for him to talk about his hurts, to smile or even laugh. He had been to a medical doctor and received anti-depressants for his condition. He'd seen a psychiatrist, several professional counselors, and prayed with several mature, Christian people, but he remained severely depressed. I explained to him that in many cases, depression is anger turned inward, so I asked him who he was angry with.

He described how his father had molested him day after day for seven years until his dad's secret was exposed. He recounted the fear and horror involved each time his father approached him when he came home from work. He said he felt guilty over never having told his mother until this family secret was discovered one night when a friend from church dropped by unexpectedly and caught Tony's dad molesting him.

Shortly after, his demented father was arrested, tried, convicted and sent to prison. Tony described always feeling dirty, plagued with lustful thoughts and having failed in three previous suicide attempts. When I finally asked him if he wanted to be free from this bondage of unresolved anger, bitterness and unforgiveness, he replied: "Yes. I do."

However, the hold that Satan had on him was so strong that Tony froze up each time he tried to pray, "God, I choose to forgive my father for molesting me." He literally could not speak those words. Quickly, I prayed aloud that the unforgiving spirit that had a grip on Tony would be bound and I quoted verse after verse about how Jesus has already purchased our freedom from sin. After a few minutes, the demonic influence that had imprisoned him left, and Tony was able to pray the prayer of forgiveness.

Tears of joy streamed down his face. He said, "It felt like something that had a hold on me was ripped out of my heart when I forgave my dad!" He knew that the Holy Spirit had healed and delivered him. All this was possible because

Tony chose to obey God's biblical commandment in Matthew 6:14-15, even though he didn't feel like forgiving. God rewarded him with a loving spirit for his faithfulness and willingness to forgive.

For those who are still unwilling to forgive someone, I understand that you're angry, that you are wounded and that the person who hurt you has made your life a living hell on earth. But are you willing to not only let that person rob you of your joy here in this life, but also to take from you any hope of being with Jesus in the next life? <u>Is holding onto your unforgiveness worth going to Hell for</u>? <u>You cannot change that person, and you cannot change the past but you have the power in Christ to change yourself now and to positively change your future</u>!

Here's an additional note of hope for you. After Paul tells us to not repay evil for evil in Romans 12:17, he continues in verse 19 to quote a passage from Deuteronomy 32:35, "'Vengeance is Mine, I will repay', says the Lord." God actually promises us two things in this passage. First, that He has removed the burden of seeking vengeance from us and secondly, that if anyone wrongs one of His own, He will mete out divine justice to the attacker. However, the phrase, "I will repay" also applies to the one wronged. Exodus (chapter 22) details the punishment for thieves: they must restore double what they stole to the owner.

Since it's not humanly possible for the one who stole your sense of self-worth, virginity, or honor to replace what he took (let alone double it), the Lord, Himself, declares that He is the one who will do so! <u>The Everlasting God, Who called the universe into existence, cares enough about you to restore your soul because you are His beloved, His chosen one, and He desires to see you whole</u>!

DYING TO OUR OLD, SINFUL WAYS

Before God can replace our childish ways of coping and displacing our hurts and anger onto others, we must be willing to surrender our old nature to Him. A dirty cup of water cannot hold clean water until it's emptied and washed first. The same applies to us. We must be willing to confess and repent of our sinful ways so God can cleanse us from the inside out. Before

He touches us through His healing hand, we must be willing to die to ourselves and let go of the poorly constructed defense mechanisms by which we used to live by.

Too often, however, Christians tend to make dying more painful than necessary. This reminds me of an old western movie where a cowboy is fatally shot in a heavy exchange of gunfire, but he seems to take forever to die. A Christian's struggle to lay down a difficult area in his life at the foot of the cross often ends up looking like a scene in one of those classic western films.

After being shot, the gunslinger staggers down the stairs, breaks through the stair rail, falls onto a series of chairs and tables, knocks down bottles, glasses, and people in the process, and finally crashes down onto the hard, wooden floor. The wounded man miraculously gets up while firing some final shots at his enemy, as he stumbles through the swinging doors of the saloon and onto the muddy streets. Then and only then can he make the claim (as if he really could after he was dead) that he died with dignity because he died with his boots on!

Usually, though, the audience has been left pondering: "Why don't you just die, for Heaven's sake, and get it over with?" I wonder what God must think when He sees us struggling over an area of sin that we've confessed and left at His altar but keep taking it back because we like our sin too much and aren't quite certain if we really want to give it up! Deliverance from a critical spirit will not come until we're truly ready to put to death its yoke of bondage. I can't help but visualize God thinking, "Just die to yourself, child, just die." Imagine how comical we must look to Him at times.

EXERCISING SELF-CONTROL

Finally, God gives us victory over a critical spirit as we choose to exercise self-control. How many times have we felt like saying something derogatory to someone and, in the end, the Holy Spirit told us "No?" More often, perhaps, than we would like to confess! A good rule of thumb to live by is: if a statement is not meant to edify another person, then it should not be spoken. An individual who has control over what he or she says is a very wise person. In fact, Proverbs 10:19 states, "In the multitude of words sin is not lacking, but he who restrains his lips is wise."

Some of us would do well to revert back to our childhood for a moment and remember when we saw the animated movie, Bambi (1942). In an opening scene in the forest, an adorable fawn, Bambi, is learning how to walk. In the process, he stumbles and falls. A young, male rabbit, notices immediately and comments, "He doesn't walk very good, does he?" His mother responds, "Thumper, what did your father tell you this morning?" Knowing that he failed in this important life lesson, he redeems himself when he says, "If you can't say something nice, don't say anything at all." [18]

How wonderful it would be if we could all practice this principle of self-restraint that begins in childhood and should continue throughout our adult lives. It would avoid a lot of unnecessary pain and heartache, build more trust in our relationships and edify our godly character. If we can't verbalize the truth in love, we should remain silent until we're able to articulate loving words of affirmation that build others up. We would all be better off by listening to Thumper's wise mother and father!

In Galatians 5:22-26, we're encouraged by the apostle Paul to not fulfill the lust of the flesh, which desires to attack innocent people, but to "walk in the Spirit" so that others can see the good work that God has done in our lives. He further states: "But the fruit of the Spirit is love, joy, peace, longsuffering, kindness, goodness, faithfulness, gentleness, self-control. Against such there is no law. And those who are Christ's have crucified the flesh with its passions and desires. If we live in the Spirit, let us also walk in the Spirit. Let us not become conceited, provoking one another, envying one another."

If we truly belong to Christ, these special qualities will be evident to all who are around us. However, when we refuse to allow the Lord full access into our lives, we, like Peter, in his moments of weakness, are guilty of denying that we even know Him before the world. Exercising self-control on a daily basis is a testimony to us and to the world that God has brought death to our critical, fearful self and replaced it with a loving spirit.

"FINALLY, MY BRETHREN..."

Our inner selves can be described this way: we are a spirit, we have a soul and we live in a body. The apostle Paul supports this in 1 Thessalonians 5:23, "Now may the God of peace Himself sanctify you completely; and may your whole spirit, soul, and body be preserved blameless at the coming of our Lord Jesus Christ." When we give our lives to Jesus, only our spirits are revived and sanctified. Our souls (our minds, wills and emotions) are still held hostage to the mindsets and habits that we developed when we practiced sinful living prior to salvation.

That's why our mental lives often resemble a giant game of tug-of-war—our fleshly desires and our spirits fight for control and our souls are the battleground where we'll either win or lose in the arena of faith. Trusting God is not an option for those who endeavor to win this battle—it's required! The Lord desires for all of His children to die to the lust of the flesh and the mental/emotional strongholds through which we revile others. It's a grueling, brutal prize fight for control and our spirit must defeat our fleshy desires if we expect to grow spiritually.

Yielding control of our lives to the Lord, however, is only the first step. In order to find true release from the oppression that binds us, we must also take control of our thoughts, "casting down arguments and every high thing that exalts itself against the knowledge of God, bringing every thought into captivity to the obedience of Christ" (2 Corinthians 10:5). Why? Because our thought lives influence our emotions, our decision-making process and, in turn, our behavior, whether good or bad. Proverbs 23:7 addresses this concept very plainly, "as he thinks in his heart, so is he" (Proverbs 23:7).

You'll never rise above the lies that others have spoken over you until you replace them with God's truth in your mind. You'll never be able to conquer the judgmental spirit that oppresses your tongue until you learn to think no evil (1 Corinthians 13:5). But even more than just controlling the negative, Philippians 4:8 tells us that we must focus our thoughts on the positive—on things that are true, noble, just, pure, and of good report.

This is what Paul meant when he talked about being

"transformed by the renewing" of our minds (Romans 12:2). That's why we must consciously choose to discipline our thoughts and emotions so they are reconciled (kept in line) with God's Word. In so doing, we'll be able to overcome any desire to wrongly judge and we'll experience a greater release and freedom to use our words to bless others instead.

You cannot be loving and judgmental at the same time—it's impossible. The Holy Spirit fights against your flesh to influence you to do the right thing, knowing there's going to be a winner every time in this heated arm wrestling match. And each time you surrender to the Lord, you grow spiritually stronger and it becomes easier to deny your carnal nature in the next battle. God has called us to suffer and that especially includes the suffering involved as we deny our flesh of its sinful pleasures.

I know that for some of you who come from a highly abusive background that this may seem like an insurmountable task, but remember what Jesus said in Luke 1:37: "For with God nothing will be impossible." Yes, our Heavenly Father is able to bring deliverance to His children in whatever area we may be struggling! It's not hopeless—the God of all hope eagerly desires to prepare His Bride, and if He says it can be done, who are we to argue? That means that healing and deliverance belong to you, mighty warrior! The promises of God are for the true Bride of Christ who will dare to live fully surrendered. And, if you're not completely surrendered, my friend, you can begin today! Isaiah 41:9-10, 13 declares,

> You whom I have taken from the ends of the
> earth, And called from its farthest regions,
> And said to you, 'You are My servant,
> I have chosen you and have not cast you away:
> Fear not, for I am with you;
> Be not dismayed, for I am your God.
> I will strengthen you,
> Yes, I will help you,
> I will uphold you with My righteous right
> hand'
> [...]
> For I, the Lord your God, will hold your right
> hand,
> Saying to you, 'Fear not, I will help you.'
> [Emphasis author's]

BEWARE OF THE TONGUE!

No man can tame the tongue, which often masquerades as good.
It is used to bless our Father and to curse our fellow man;
It's full of deadly poison! Its venom must be understood;
While it speaks evil curses, it also lends a helping hand.

How have you been influenced by such a morbid host?
What lies do you speak in the messages that you send?
Beware of the arrogant heart that causes you to boast:
It aims to inflict pain and devour all your friends.

As you take time to reflect on the days of your youth,
What do you remember that still bothers you today?
What did you do to compromise the way of the truth?
Has unforgiveness, child, caused you to go astray?

Perhaps you became a victim when you made mistakes—
Were your parents harsh in pointing out the error of your ways?
Can you still hear the screaming that causes you to shake?
It's time to stop the beatings that haunt you to this day.

A whiner, a complainer is that what you've become—
Contaminating other people with the force of a gun?
The battle you have fought for control of your tongue
Is one you must not take lightly, for the war has just begun.

Prayer is the key that unlocks healing in your life
Where God will fill your desolate places and grant you good
    health.
With the power of His love, like a surgeon with his knife,
He'll heal your open wounds and cut out your critical self.

How long will you wrestle with God in a match you cannot win?
He wants your confession for the children that you've slain—
For the lives you have destroyed through your malicious tongue
that sins. A trail of blood of the innocent cries, "Help me! I've
    been maimed!"

"You call yourself a Christian, but commit murder in your heart.
You lack patience with others, yet you expect it in return.

How long will you act as Satan's puppet, shooting deadly darts?
Cease from these killings now, child, is what your heart must
   learn.

You alone cannot tame the monster that wants to steal your soul.
Where you have lacked mercy, love, understanding and grace,
I will pour out My Spirit and fill the empty, loveless hole
That has polluted your well and left it there to waste.

Cease from defiling My temple in you and all the others,
And no longer bear false witness against your neighbors,
Or you'll be consumed when you devour your sister and brother.
Consecrate yourself now before your heart and mouth waver.

The hateful and unforgiving live in misery,
But My own crucify their flesh with its passions and desires.
Only Jesus, My Son, can forgive your sins and set you free:
Beware of the tongue, My child, for it is a deadly fire!"

CHAPTER FOUR

"SURELY HE BORE OUR SORROWS..."

...Fear not, for I have redeemed you; I have called you by your
name; You are Mine. When you pass through the waters,
I will be with you...they shall not overflow you.
When you walk through the fire, you shall not
be burned, nor shall the flame
scorch you. For I am the
Lord your God, the
Holy One of
Israel, your
Savior...
(Isaiah 43:1-3)

The Lord's promises are unfailing because His character
is unchanging. His love and compassion for us goes so far
beyond what we could ever imagine! And yet, there come times
for all of us when the burdens we carry look so overwhelming
that we may feel our Heavenly Father has forgotten us or doesn't
hear us anymore. We may feel like second-class citizens in
the kingdom of Heaven: we know we have the assurance
of salvation, but God only seems to speak to everyone else
and answer their prayers while our requests appear to go
unanswered.

Have you grown weary in your heart from waiting on
the Lord to give you an answer as the months or years pass by?
Have you ever wondered, "What's the point to all this, anyway?"
You are not alone! One of the most difficult challenges in life,
regardless of one's age, is to steadfastly endure when trials
attempt to drown you in sorrow. People either grow weaker or
stronger when tribulation strikes. There is no middle ground;
trials will either draw us closer to God or push us farther away,
for they truly test the resiliency of our faith.

Sometimes, when we've begun to take His love for
granted, the Lord will not allow us to feel His presence to help
us realize how much we need Him. In those times, He wants

to stir up in us the same joyful eagerness of fellowship that we experienced when we first fell in love with Him. Just as a marriage will not thrive if the romantic embers of courtship are not gently kindled, so, too, will the passion that fuels our relationship with God gradually fade if it isn't steadily nurtured.

When we become too distracted by the cares of this world and the daily grind of making a living, our loving Lord will often use that "dry season" of not feeling His presence or hearing His voice as a means to spur us on to fervently seek Him again. He also uses those times of waiting to strengthen us and to bring us from the immaturity of a child, who must have the answer now, to the maturity of His Bride, who is willing to wait patiently for the Wedding Day, trusting wholeheartedly that her Groom will not fail her.

"WHEN YOU WALK THROUGH THE WATERS..."

Sometimes, God, in His infinite wisdom of knowing what is best for us, allows us to walk through troubling situations that He could have easily prevented by His power. Why?

> ...we also glory in tribulations, knowing
> that tribulation produces perseverance; and
> perseverance, character; and character, hope.
> Now hope does not disappoint, because the
> love of God has been poured out in our hearts
> by the Holy Spirit who was given to us.
> (Romans 5:3-5)

When we can meet those circumstances with calm endurance and hope, our ability to trust the Lord will increase and produce spiritual stamina in us. Even more importantly, the delays we often experience of waiting for Him to answer our prayers will stretch our capacity to trust Him. Adversity trains us for higher levels of faith and for being in God's glorious presence as He manifests Himself to us in new ways.

He purposely delays responding and takes us beyond our human deadlines for answers so that, through our waiting and believing, He can make a little more room in our hearts to pour Himself into. When we can look at these dark valleys through God's eyes, we can see He's able to work all things together for our good (whether we agree with Him or not), using them to perfect us as His Bride while He draws us closer to Himself (Romans 8:28).

How often have we eagerly prayed, "Lord, take me into Your presence," but, when He sends us the fiery trials which bring us closer to Him, refused them like spoiled children? Challenging times are God's grace to us: they allow us to live in His glory as we pursue Him when we're desperate for answers. But, when we have a fleshly (carnal or immature) reaction to adversity instead, we miss the purposes of God and forfeit the miracles that He could have done as well as the anointing and the opportunity that we could have received to mature more spiritually.

Carnal Christians are guided by their thoughts and negative feelings (fear, unresolved anger, impatience and discouragement) as opposed to mature Christians who are led by the Holy Spirit. Isaiah 43:1-3 addresses this,

> But now, thus says the Lord, who created you, O Jacob, and He who formed you, O Israel: Fear not, for I have redeemed you; I have called you by your name; you are Mine. When you pass through the waters, I will be with you; and through the rivers, they shall not overflow you. When you walk through the fire, you shall not be burned, nor shall the flame scorch you. For I am the Lord your God, the Holy One of Israel, your Savior... [Emphasis author's]

God says He'll be with us when we suffer through our afflictions. The alternative is that if we refuse to go through them by using such controlling behaviors as avoiding, blaming and manipulating, then we'll never know how to walk in God's magnificent presence or see His mighty hand move on our behalf.

The fruit of the Spirit often grows during tribulation. When someone abuses us, we have the opportunity to respond in the Spirit by blessing and praying for that individual, the result being kindness, patience and self-control. Yes, our loving, Heavenly Father will sometimes purposely put us in trying circumstances, or in a situation with a difficult person! But if we have a fleshly reaction and pray only for deliverance ("Lord, get me out of here!"), then all we do is reinforce our own carnality. We remain in an immature, spiritual state. As a result, we find we did not learn anything from that trial.

AS IRON SHARPENS IRON, SO ONE MAN SHARPENS ANOTHER

When I was working as a counselor in a school setting, I received an abusive phone call from a parent whose child had recently been suspended. Besides using words that I wouldn't dare repeat, this father threatened to bring a lawsuit against me and the school for the way he felt the case was handled. At this point, I had a choice: would I react immaturely by giving in to anger, panic and blaming or would I respond in the Spirit?

Even while this man continued his out-of-control tirade as I held the phone far from my ear to protect my hearing, I quickly asked the Lord, "Father, what's going on?" All I heard in reply was the Holy Spirit saying with a chuckle, "Testing, testing, 1, 2, 3, testing!" Suddenly, the whole situation seemed comical and absolutely absurd. There was no way the parent could make good on any of his threats, since we were covered by the law.

Pastor, author and speaker, Graham Cooke, once shared:

> Nobody made you angry. You chose to get angry. You could've done the opposite; you could've moved in the Spirit; you could've prayed for those who were persecuting you; you could've blessed those who were abusing you; you could've loved your enemy at that point, but no, you chose to get angry. That's your sin, nobody else's... nobody makes you

angry, nobody makes you resentful, nobody
makes you feel rejected: those are choices
that we make for ourselves. You could've
chosen something else, because you have all
of Heaven at your disposal [as well as] the
Holy Spirit Who is stamping the image and the
nature of Jesus in your life. [19]

I passed this test because, as I walked through the
fire, I chose to not sin in my anger, to not pick up the flaming
darts of slander and accusation which were temptingly
supplied by the enemy. Instead, I patiently put my hands
into the hands of the Holy Spirit. Because I trusted Him, I
felt His sustaining presence giving me joy and peace beyond
understanding (Philippians 4:7).

We must remember that Jesus was despised and
rejected, as we will be on occasion, because God uses those
opportunistic trials to purge and purify us so we can become
more like Him. It is comforting to know that since the Lord
passed these same kinds of trials (Hebrews 4:15) that He will
empower us to pass them, too.

"COUNT IT ALL JOY, MY BRETHREN..."

Along the same lines, our loving, Heavenly Father
will often put us right in the middle of a problematic situation
or allow the enemy of our souls to afflict us in a limited way,
as He did with Job. As a young Christian, I could never
understand why a "just and loving God" would allow him
to suffer so much. I chose to not finish reading this story
because what happened to him in the first two chapters was
more than I could bear.

This really messed up my theology of who I thought
the Lord was and what I believed He was like. Later, while
I was reading through the book of Ezekiel, I found our
Heavenly Father proclaimed not once, not twice, but three
times that Job was one of the most righteous men in the Old
Testament (Ezekiel 14:14,18,20). I quickly learned that we
are all called to partake in the sufferings and blessings of
Christ.

Unfortunately, when the tide of circumstances suddenly turns against us, as it did with Job, we sometimes question what God is doing or if He even knows what's happening. Because we periodically interpret our situations simply by what we see and feel, and because we don't trust the Lord completely, we accuse Almighty God of abusing and neglecting His children. This is an accusation that He does not take lightly!

We see God's swift judgment on this kind of attitude in the book of Numbers:

> Then they [the Hebrews] journeyed from
> Mount Hor by the way of the Red Sea...
> and the soul of the people became very
> discouraged [impatient] on the way. And the
> people spoke against God and against Moses:
> "Why have you brought us up out of Egypt to
> die in the wilderness? For there is no food and
> no water, and our soul loathes this worthless
> bread [manna]." So the Lord sent fiery
> serpents among the people, and they bit the
> people; and many of the people of Israel died.
> (Numbers 21:4-6)

The message is very clear: God will not allow an unbelieving, murmuring spirit to infect His Bride. After all the goodness He has poured out on us, and after all the miracles He has done on our behalf, the most hurtful, spiteful accusation we could make against Him is to say He doesn't care about His children. This is merely blaming and self-pity.

So, what can we do so we don't make the same mistakes as our ancestors did? Rather than giving in to negative coping mechanisms such as blaming God for our trial in much the same way that Adam and Eve did when they ate the forbidden fruit, we need to be honest with the Lord. We need to pour our hearts out to Him in a spirit of brokenness and humility and let Him know we feel weak and abandoned by Him. Remember that even Jesus in Mark 15:34 cried out, "My God, My God, why have You forsaken Me?" The Lord understands how we feel.

He wants us to bear our hearts to Him when we're hurting. If we're lacking in faith and struggling with doubt, He wants to hear about it so He can help us work through it so we don't develop a critical spirit. This is humility and greatly pleases God (Psalm 51:17). The Holy Spirit is available to comfort us whenever we need Him. Don't hesitate in revealing to Him exactly how you feel.

He longs for His children to come to Him when we're hurting so He can hug us with His loving arms. This reminds me of when I took my nephew, Jerry Gutierrez, to church with me when he was around seven years old. During the service, Pastor Glenn Cole of Capital Christian Center in Sacramento, California, announced that he sensed that many people were hurting emotionally and needed a special touch by God. So, he prayed that people would literally feel God give them a hug.

As I turned to my nephew, I saw tears streaming down his face. Afterwards, I asked him if he would share with me why he was crying. He replied, "Uncle Victor, I felt God give me a hug." God truly understands when we're feeling weak and need His loving comfort. We serve a God of love and He longs to fellowship with us all the time.

Jesus knows that we're not going to walk in faith 100% of the time because of our sinful nature. That's when He expects us to come before Him with a broken spirit so He can strengthen us from within. I have a friend who is brutally honest with the Lord. In fact, he tells me that sometimes He feels so frustrated with God when he's struggling through a trial that He throws His Bible at Him! He tells me, "I know the Lord can take it, Vic. Then, I go pick it up, ask the Lord to forgive me and get back to praying." The Lord loves this kind of genuineness, although I wouldn't do this all the time because replacing one Bible after another will get expensive after a while.

In contrast with the Israelites, Job, our amazing role model, overcame adversity because in all his pain and sorrow, he did not curse God. The Lord blessed and restored to him what he had lost because he had spoken rightly of Him and prayed for his "friends" who had tried to undermine his faith (Job 42:7-11). In other words, this humble servant responded in the Spirit, allowing God to help him bear his burdens, instead of reacting carnally. James 5:11 says, "Indeed we count them blessed who endure. You have heard of the perseverance of Job and seen the end intended by the Lord—that the Lord is very compassionate and merciful."

"FOLLOW ME"

However, if God's ideas of compassion and mercy seem very different from ours, that's only because His priorities and ways of looking at things are very dissimilar from ours, too. As Graham Cooke once emphasized, "God doesn't want to make us better; He wants to make us deader!" [20] Jesus said, "Whoever desires to come after Me, let him deny himself, and take up his cross, and follow Me. For whoever desires to save his life will lose it, but whoever loses his life for My sake...will save it" (Mark 8:34-35).

Jesus has the authority to require total surrender of us not only because He is God, but because He did it first! "He humbled Himself and became obedient to the point of death, even the death of the cross" (Philippians 2:8). This is what Isaiah 53:4 means when this prophet writes, "He bore our sorrows": even though He is God, He was every bit as human as we are, going through the same trials and temptations that we experience, all designed to bring Him to the point of dying to fleshly desires (Matthew 26:39). That's how He was able to get to the place where He could say "Most assuredly, I say to you, the Son can do nothing of Himself, but what He sees the Father do; for whatever He does, the Son also does in like manner" (John 5:19).

His priority now is to make us like Himself and to grow us into maturity. Once we learn to die to our fleshly desires by responding in the Spirit instead of reacting carnally, we'll be able to move into the higher realms of the Spirit and draw closer to the Lord.

But, because of our Fiancé's compassion and mercy, even though we fail His tests, God frequently allows us to take them over again. But don't count on this because we don't always know when the Lord will give us a second or third chance. First time obedience is always best because it not only shows the Lord how much we love Him, but it may also shorten our suffering.

Please understand that God isn't up in Heaven saying, "This is for your own good, so there!" He feels our hurt and does not delight in making us wait for relief. However, there is an essential link between pain and passion: if we were to go through life without anguish, what reason would we have to yearn passionately for God, or how would we be able to respond compassionately to others? Pain has the capacity to produce greater passion for the Lord and compassion for those who are hurting in the heart of an obedient Christian.

When Lazarus was dying (John, chapter 11), Jesus stayed two additional days where He was before going to see him, knowing full well what the outcome would be. He chose to delay coming even though He knew it would cause great agony and grief to people whom He counted as dear friends. Why? So that more people would see the greater miracle and realize He was the Messiah.

It's important to understand that "Jesus loved Martha and her sister and Lazarus" (John 11:5), and that He had stayed at their home before (Luke 10:38-42). They might have even accompanied Him on some of His journeys. They were special to Him and knew Jesus well.

When He finally came and spoke to Mary and Martha, He had two reactions to their grief: He groaned in the Spirit and He wept (John 11:33-35). He cried because He was touched by their heartache, but He groaned in Himself ("embrimaomai" in the Greek) and was troubled because He was frustrated that they "didn't get it," even though He had clearly told Martha that her brother would rise again (verse 23).

God groans over us in the same way when we're slow to trust Him. He takes no pleasure in prolonging our misery, but is pleased when we learn how to rest in His promises and love Him more intimately through our affliction, even as Jesus used adversity to pull Himself closer to the Father. If we can learn to wait upon the Lord (Isaiah 40:31) while we allow His love to help us face our hurts and fears during our trials, not only will we receive healing ourselves, but we'll also be used by Him to minister restoration to others, just as Jesus did.

Also, ministering to someone while you're hurting is one of the highest forms of spiritual warfare you can engage in and it will quickly usher in healing in your life. It's very powerful and Satan doesn't want you to discover this spiritual truth because he knows you'll skyrocket to a higher level of spiritual maturity when you apply it. This causes great fear in your enemy!

I recall when I was working as a high school counselor at Stagg High School in Stockton, California in 2006 that I was going through one of the most painful trials of my life. My heart was broken because of a broken relationship. I was tempted often to stay home so I wouldn't have to face my responsibilities at work, but I chose to persevere.

As I prayed during my drive to work one day, I experienced closeness with God that I had never sensed before. I felt like the Lord was literally holding me in His arms and telling me that He was going to help me walk through this very arduous trial, and He did! I felt His strength rise up within me prior to arriving at work. My entire countenance changed and I went from feeling extremely sad to feeling very hopeful within seconds after I began praying.

Later that day, a student came into my office and vividly described how her heart was broken because her parents had recently divorced. She painted a distressing picture of how much she missed her father and was deeply saddened that her mom and dad were unable to work out their marital problems. She agonized over feeling guilty and responsible for her parents' failed marriage.

As I listened to her, I felt the Holy Spirit's presence. I sensed that He was trying to wrap this precious girl in a blanket of love as I shared truths about the dynamics of divorce that helped to free her from false guilt that she was wrongly carrying. She received her breakthrough in much the same way that I experienced mine earlier in my drive to work.

When we finished talking, I could tell her heart was no longer heavy and she was feeling much better. Her face glowed, she smiled, her shoulders no longer drooped and she spoke with hope and a greater resolve in overcoming adversity. God reminded me that when we take our minds off of ourselves and give to others that His presence invades our lives and He begins to do surgery on the hearts of those who need it, including our own.

We have more strength than we realize, even when we're heartbroken, when we put our trust in the Lord. As I affirmed and comforted this distraught teenager, I could feel God's presence removing another layer of hurt from my wounded spirit. The Lord performs miracles within us when we minister to others, despite our shattered hearts.

Satan becomes very angry when we engage in this kind of spiritual warfare because he thinks he has defeated us when we appear too weak to fight back. But he quickly forgets that God carries us when we cry out to Him out of desperation, brokenness and a pure heart. The Apostle Paul spoke about this in 2 Corinthians 12:9-10. It reads, "...My grace is sufficient for you, for My strength is made perfect in weakness...I take pleasure in infirmities, in reproaches, in needs, in persecutions, in distresses, for Christ's sake. For when I am weak, then I am strong."

"BLESSED ARE THE PEACEMAKERS"

Many of us know the story of when Jesus was asleep in the boat in Luke 8:22-25. He and all His disciples were crossing the Sea of Galilee when a fierce storm descended on them and the boat started to fill with water. The men panicked and woke Him, declaring they were all going to die. Jesus stood up, rebuked the storm, and reproved His disciples for not exercising their faith. But how many of us realize they went through this test twice?

In the meantime, Jesus led them through some amazing circumstances to strengthen their faith so they would have a better opportunity of passing this trial the second time. They saw the Gadarene demoniac delivered (Luke 8:26-39), they were present when the woman with "an issue of blood" was healed (Luke 8:43-47), they waited while Jairus' daughter was raised from the dead (Luke 8:54), they were sent out two by two, exercising the power to cast out demons and heal the sick (Mark 6:13) and they saw five thousand people fed (Matthew 14:13-21).

Unfortunately, they still didn't understand. John tells us that after they had picked up all the fragments of fish and bread, the disciples were about to take Jesus by force to make Him king (John 6:15). Matthew and Mark both record that He encouraged His disciples to get into a boat to go ahead of Him to the other side (Matthew 14:22 and Mark 6:45), while He went up to a mountain to pray. The Bible doesn't tell us what He and His Father were talking about, but Pastor Graham Cooke believes that Jesus was likely asking Him to test the disciples' faith by making the waves really big this time! [21]

This is a pattern of how the Lord often works in our lives: He reveals to us our calling and purpose ("Go to the other side of the lake"), but on the way there, the opposition comes. Will we react in the flesh or respond in the Spirit? Remember, God will never ask us to do something that we can't do! If He tells us to go to the other side, then we can rest assured that we'll get there.

But when we lose sight of the Lord's promises and focus on our problems instead, the warfare will become so fierce that our carnal struggles will lead us nowhere. This is also God's grace to us: He uses tribulation to reveal what's in our hearts and just how much ground Satan has in us. Once we receive His revelation, it's up to us to rise up and take that territory back for God and for ourselves.

Even though Jesus saw His disciples in a vision "straining at rowing, for the wind was against them" (Mark 6:48), He stayed on the mountain for six more hours, praying until about three a.m. ("the fourth watch of the night"—same verse). Why did He wait? Like a parent patiently waiting for a child to complete a new task, Pastor Cooke believes He wanted to give them an opportunity to respond in the Spirit by taking authority over the storm even as they had seen Him do before.[22]

Finally, when Jesus came to them by walking on the water, He found them troubled (Matthew 14:26) and afraid (John 6:19). We cannot bring serenity to this world unless we live in the realm of God's peace; Jesus was able to calm the tempest because He spoke in agreement with what was already within Him! How can we hope to quiet any kind of thunderstorm that surrounds us when anxiety or lack of trust in the Lord prevents us from entering into God's rest (Hebrews 4:9)? Instead of being peacemakers and part of the solution, we become part of the problem.

So, let me encourage you in this area because some people may feel false guilt or condemnation when they hear they need to have God's peace while they feel anxious or nervous. God knows your unique circumstances and the reasons why you may struggle with apprehension. To overcome this culprit, you must choose to put your faith in God, regardless of whether a peaceful feeling accompanies your decision. Some people struggle with anxious feelings more than others, due to a chemical imbalance, but they must still learn to trust the Lord.

If you feel peaceful after choosing to submit your cares to God, it's a bonus. Praise God! Often, peaceful emotions will follow your decision to surrender your deepest fears to the Lord. Though the Lord will speak to you through your emotions at times, don't allow this realm alone to be your guide. The Holy Spirit is your Helper, your Comforter (John 14:26) and He will guide you into all truth (John 16:13).

Let's contrast the disciples' reactions to their storms with Paul's response in Acts 27:13-44. Instead of panicking as the twelve were after just six hours, Paul endured two weeks of rough sailing! Because of his attitude of peace and trust that the Lord would fulfill the promise that none would perish—given to him in an angelic visitation (verses 22-25)—even the sailors with him "were all encouraged, and also took food themselves" (verse 36). In the end, because of Paul's peaceful trust, "they all escaped safely to land" (verse 44).

The measure of a person's maturity is found by the amount of opposition it takes to discourage him and get his eyes off the Lord. [23] Peter did finally understand this concept, and he expounds on this in 1 Peter 4:12-13:

> Beloved, do not think it strange concerning the
> fiery trial which is to try you, as though some
> strange thing happened to you; but rejoice

to the extent that you partake of Christ's
sufferings, that when His glory is revealed,
you may also be glad with exceeding joy.

The weapons with which the enemy wars against us
are the very evils that keep us locked in our self-made prison
of surviving: fear, anxiety, worry, unbelief, helplessness,
self-pity, blaming and rationalizing. When we give in to
these deadly enemies, Satan keeps us in the realm of the soul
(the mind, will and emotions), and he often wins the battle
there. But, if we can choose to "walk by faith, not by sight"
(2 Corinthians 5:7), we'll fight the battle from the realm of
the Spirit and faith. This is where the Promised Land is and
we should aim to live there every day.

Then, we'll have access to the one weapon that
frustrates the enemy the most: trust! Proverbs 3:5-6 reminds
us to "Trust in the Lord with all your heart, and lean not on
your own understanding; in all your ways acknowledge Him,
and He shall direct your paths." Submitting our lives to God
and walking in His rest and tranquility is a shield that the
enemy of our souls can't penetrate. And our enemy hates
that! Why? There is nothing more dangerous to Satan than
a faith-filled Christian who walks in God's peace, is full of
the joy of the Lord and laughs at fear because his trust in the
Lord is true and pure. This kind of faith is contagious and
can inspire other believers to follow him into the Promised
Land. So, the key to victory is to fight Satan on God's terms
and conditions—with a Christ-like mindset.

LOOK FOR THE TABLE

Graham Cooke once shared a dream he experienced
at a conference. In the dream, he was with other Christians
in a fierce battle with the forces of darkness. People were
wounded, weak and exhausted, but the enemy withdrew
before them and fled. A faint cry of victory rose up from
God's army, even as many of them had to lean on their
swords for support because they were so fatigued from
warfare that they could barely stand.

Then, he looked to the right and saw a massive,
hostile battalion marching straight towards them. With fierce

determination, he pulled his sword up to his shoulder and decided that though this looked like the end, he was going to take out as many of the enemy's troops as he could before he went down!

Suddenly, the Lord stood next to him dressed as a maitre d', complete with a towel draped over His arm, and said, "Will you be having the melon or the soup?"

Astonished and without taking his eyes off the advancing host, Graham exclaimed, "But Lord, the enemy is going to overwhelm us! Just look!"

Again, Jesus asked him, "So, will you be having the melon or the soup?"

"But, Lord, we're vastly outnumbered; we're going to be annihilated!"

Jesus replied, "You know, Graham, you're really looking a bit faint, and you ought to keep your strength up. Will you be having the melon or the soup?"

Even though the opposition was getting so close that he could now see their eyes, Graham forced himself to look behind him to where the Lord was. There, right on the field of combat was a huge banqueting table, piled high with every kind of healthy food imaginable. The dream abruptly ended and he woke up laughing and declaring, "Okay, Lord, I'll have the melon!" [24]

If this seems strange, remember the 23rd Psalm: "Yea, though I walk through the valley of the shadow of death, I will fear no evil; for You are with me...You prepare a table before me in the presence of my enemies..." (verses 4-5). God is so supremely confident of Who He is and of His ability to deliver us that all the hordes of Hell do not concern Him. Yes, we are in a battle, and yes, we'll have to fight, but He wants us to fight from His perspective and with supreme confidence in who He is and in His ability to deliver us.

When we take our eyes off the enemy and put our focus on the Lord, we'll be refreshed and renewed. Exodus 14:13 reminds us that we are called to "...not be afraid. Stand still, and see the salvation of the Lord..." That is the rest that we should strive to enter: knowing we are seated in Heavenly places in Christ Jesus (Ephesians 2:6). When you find rest, you enter the Promised Land.

PATIENTLY ENDURING TO OBTAIN GOD'S PROMISES

Complete healing from our past takes time, not necessarily because God moves slowly according to our timelines, but because we so frequently stand in His way, or insist that we can do a better, faster job. Fear does not wait, but acts on its own and very hastily. Patience, on the other hand, waits for God's timing, is often part of the healing and deliverance process, and is how we show the Lord that we love Him as we learn to persevere.

We chose to wait on God to deliver us from our sinful lifestyles when we gave our lives to Christ. It is no different as we grow in our daily walk with Him. God still expects us to seek Him through prayer to meet all of our needs. In fact, Lamentations 3:25-26 reveals that, "The Lord is good to those who wait for Him, to the soul who seeks Him. It is good that one should hope and wait quietly for the salvation of the Lord." Micah 7:7 states, "Therefore I will look to the Lord; I will wait for the God of my salvation; My God will hear me."

Patiently persevering is an act of trusting our Heavenly Father even in the most perilous circumstances or when our flesh would rather take the lead. When we endure, we learn how to love God in a deeper way and fear is slain before we give it an opportunity to grow its horrifying roots in us. Therefore, when we're able to exercise patience in trying conditions or when we're challenged by abrasive people, this is a sign that the Holy Spirit is dynamically moving in us and that we're growing in our walk of faith.

"BE NOT AFRAID; ONLY BELIEVE"

Edwin Louis Cole, a pastor, lecturer and author, states, "Our faith is imperfect. Human faith has doubt built into it. Divine faith has no doubt. The faith that God wants us to use in our lives is not our human faith, but His faith that is in us by the indwelling of the Spirit of Jesus." [25]

However, this kind of faith requires trust. Our relationship with God demands that we believe He is in control, and that He has our best interests at heart, even when circumstances seem chaotic. Hebrews 11:6 states, "…without faith it is impossible to please Him…"

This kind of trust pleases God. We must choose to be vulnerable, to relinquish control and submit all of our hurts, needs, wants and dreams to the Lord, even if He chooses to answer us in a different way than what we anticipated.

David Wilkerson expounds on this further:

You may object, saying, "Almost every time Jesus performed a miracle, He told people, 'Only believe!'" Yet in each instance He said this to people who had come to the end of all hope—who had lost faith in everything else... Paul did not speak of having faith until he had lost all confidence in his flesh...Yet saving, justifying faith involves more than [this]... It also involves submitting your whole life to Christ with all your heart. It includes a repentance that says, "Jesus, I've got nothing to offer You. I am nothing and I have nothing. I come to submit to Your Lordship!" [26]

Shadrach, Meshach and Abednego came to such a place in their walks with God. King Nebuchadnezzar had built a giant statue of gold and required that everyone bow down and worship it. However, the third chapter of Daniel reminds us that these three refused to do so, even though death in the fiery furnace awaited them for defying this wicked leader.

As they stood before this ruler, they realized there was nothing they could do to save themselves, and there was no one but God Almighty Who could deliver them. They had to completely submit themselves to the Lord, for they had no "arm of flesh" in which they could trust (2 Chronicles 32:8). They declared in Daniel 3:17-18, "…our God whom we serve is able to deliver us from the burning fiery furnace, and He will deliver us from your hand, O king. But if not...we do not serve your gods, nor will we worship the gold image which you have set up" [emphasis author's].

It would have been easy to disobey the king if they had known God was going to save them, but they had to take one giant step beyond that and decide they would remain faithful, even if the Lord allowed them to die. Faith requires so much more than just trusting God when everything goes well! It is the kind of faith which states: "Though He slay me, yet will I trust Him" (Job 13:15). This kind of trust pleases the Lord because it reverently whispers, "I surrender every ounce of my being to you, Lord."

GOD'S HOPE DOES NOT DISAPPOINT

The hope that God gives us as His children is beyond the hope of a worldly person, who, in reality, has none. We have the eager expectation that the Lord will answer our prayers because we belong to Him. Listen to the hope that King David speaks of in Psalm 16:8-1:

> I have set the Lord always before me; because
> He is at my right hand I shall not be moved.
> Therefore, my heart is glad, and my glory
> rejoices; my flesh also will rest in hope...You
> will show me the path of life; in your presence
> is fullness of joy; at your right hand are
> pleasures forevermore. [Emphasis author's]

Romans 5:5 declares, "Now hope does not disappoint, because the love of God has been poured out in our hearts by the Holy Spirit who was given to us." Fear (Satan) disappoints and destroys; love (God) ignites and satisfies our souls. Jesus gives us hope!

I'm reminded of a trying time I faced during the second year of my marriage. My wife became pregnant with our first child, we had just bought our first home and I received a lay-off notice from my job shortly after. I spent about a month applying for work at various school districts, but I didn't receive even a single phone call for an interview. Needless to say, my faith began to waver. After a few sleepless, worry-filled nights, the Lord led me to His Word.

He showed me that I had failed to trust Him to provide for me and my family.

I realized that I had disappointed Him. How? Instead of waiting on Him to grant me peace during this trial, I gave in to fear, worry, doubt, and unbelief. As I repented of these sins, God assured me that I could always count on Him to help me, since He and His Word never change. Hebrews 13:8 declares: "Jesus Christ is the same yesterday, today, and forever." I was not practicing the principle of trust outlined in Philippians 4:6. It reads, "Do not be anxious over nothing but in everything with prayer and supplication and thanksgiving, let your requests be made known to God and the peace of God which surpasses all understanding will guard your hearts and minds in Christ Jesus."

Though I was aware that school districts throughout the state were experiencing budget cuts, that my child would soon be born, that my position would soon be eliminated, and that there was no visible hope in sight, God gave me hope where I was not able to see it myself as He taught me the value of waiting patiently on Him. A month before my contract ended, the Lord blessed me with a school counseling position that paid twenty-five percent more than my former job, which would help to provide for the beautiful, new addition to our family: my son, Joshua.

Shortly after, as I was reading my Bible, a scripture stood out to me. Philippians 4:19 read: "And my God shall supply all your need according to His riches in glory by Christ Jesus." God confirmed to me through His Word that He always proves Himself faithful, especially when we have our backs against a wall and don't know what to do.

As a result of this burdensome trial, my Heavenly Father strengthened me. I've learned to trust and wait on Him through His Word more than ever because of this experience and realized I would not have grown spiritually had He not allowed me to suffer through this stressful test. Psalm 71:5 reminds us that "You are my hope, O Lord God; You are my trust from my youth." As we learn to wait upon God, we find there is no greater faith than to hope in the Lord. God's hope does not disappoint!

IMPATIENCE REVEALS YOUR TRUE HEART

Conversely, impatient people do whatever is necessary to not only make their present circumstances favorable, but to <u>avoid</u> any suffering that accompanies the character-building process the Lord is attempting to build within them. They would rather remain in their familiar, fleshly, angry, impatient state because they're not willing to pay the price required to develop mature faith.

Impatient people are constantly frustrated. When God calls them to be still and wait on Him to move in a given area in their lives, they often rationalize He has forgotten about them and that it's time to take matters into their own hands. We fall short repeatedly because we're human, a work in progress, and are continually learning how to deal with spiritual attacks.

1 Samuel chapter 13 tells us about the time King Saul was waiting for Samuel, the prophet, to come to Gilgal to offer a sacrifice to God before attacking the Philistines. Samuel had told Saul he would meet him there in eight days, but as the time passed, the king's army became distressed, hid themselves, and scattered. He waited a week for Samuel to come, but Saul became impatient and offered the sacrifice himself (1 Samuel 13:9-10).

Shortly after, Samuel showed up and saw that Saul had committed a great evil. God told him through this prophet that his kingdom would be taken from him because he failed to trust and obey the Lord. This grave error would eventually cost him his life as well as the lives of all his sons (1 Samuel 31:1-10).

When God, as your heart surgeon, is performing surgery on you, His patient, what is your attitude like? When He tells you to be still and trust the work of His hands, do you give Him advice on the best way to remedy an area of concern? Do you complain and ask Him what's taking so long because you have other matters to attend to?

Do you remind Him you have talents that are worth applying here on His operating table, as if He were lacking expertise in anything? These are signs of a fearful, controlling person who doesn't truly trust the Lord to do badly-needed character-building. If we haven't learned to be still while God is working on us, we'll experience unnecessary pain instead of peace while the Master Surgeon chisels away at the rough edges of our delicate hearts.

Every problematic situation we find ourselves in comes complete with a provision for our growth and blessing, but if we have our eyes fixed only on the problem, we won't be able to see a way out. Why? Our vision will be clouded by needless worry and stress when we don't trust the Lord to carry us through stormy weather. <u>When we're impatient, we fight against the Holy Spirit and sabotage our healing and deliverance process</u>.

If you struggle with impatience, God is faithful to meet you where you're at. Tell Him that you're short on patience and that you need help. Humble yourself by acknowledging your weakness and He'll extend you the grace to endure the fiery trial you're facing. As you seek Him, He'll reveal to you the core issues behind your impatient demeanor so you can face any fears or stressors that contribute to your angry disposition. Once you courageously face your inner demons, you'll win the battle over the dark side and the fruit of patience will manifest itself as your reward.

To illustrate, I began having nightmares when I was in college over the many bullies who had abused me throughout my childhood. This continued for years until I gave my life to Christ when I turned twenty-five. At that time, the Lord showed me the reason why I was struggling with impatience and over-reacting when faced with stressful situations was because I had unresolved anger. The Holy Spirit revealed to me that I needed to forgive the hoodlums who made my childhood a living hell.

As I realized that unforgiveness was robbing me of my peace and joy, I asked the Lord to give me the strength to forgive my enemies. This did not happen overnight. It was a process, and when I was finally able to surrender the hatred that had kept me in an emotional prison, I experienced a release, a freedom that I had not known before. It felt like chains came off of my heart as I felt God's healing touch transform me from the inside out.

Learning to calmly wait is one of the most difficult lessons you'll ever face. You will suffer as you allow the Lord to mold you, but the pain will be worth the gain. The valuable lessons you'll learn during this pruning time will be critical in your struggle to gain the patience you need to secure victory in your time of testing. If you're willing to pay the price for maturity, then you'll learn to shed your unhealthy coping mechanisms that simply feed into your impatient temperament and keep you trapped inside a dungeon of fear that won't allow you to face your emotional pain.

Patience that's birthed in fiery trials, however, will usher you into the Promised Land where you'll discover peace, truth and unwavering trust that truly pleases the heart of God. These valuable jewels are worth waiting for because not only are they hard core proof of your desire to face the truth about your character flaws, but they showcase your new-found patient demeanor and the genuineness of your faith. This pleases your Heavenly Father and brings Him glory because you shine like the sun when you rightly represent Him (1 Peter 1:7).

"WE COUNT THEM BLESSED WHO ENDURE"

When Jesus gives us a vision or a dream, and tells us to wait, we can rest assured that something good is coming, if we can endure the times of testing and maturing that prepare us for what He intends. When Joseph was seventeen, he had dreams that he would be a ruler and that many people would bow down to him (Genesis 37), but it was thirteen years before God's Word to him came to pass at age thirty (Genesis 41:46). Along the way, he had to patiently endure the shame of being sold into slavery, the disgrace of being falsely accused, and the despair of being thrown into prison many miles away from the land of his youth.

Moses felt the call to leadership when he learned of his true identity in the second chapter of Exodus. But his impatient attempt to free his people by murdering an

Egyptian slave-driver (in verse twelve) forced him to spend the next forty years exiled from the palace life. He lived as a shepherd in the wilderness before God fulfilled His promise to free the Hebrews (Acts 7:23-36).

When Jesus directed His disciples to tarry in Jerusalem for the coming of the Holy Spirit, they had no idea how long they would have to wait (Luke 24:49). The city authorities were still hostile toward them and the people were stirred up with the debate over whether He had truly risen or if His followers had stolen His body. It may very well have been an anxious time for them to remain in a place so unfriendly in light of recent events. But they had to stay there for forty days before the Holy Spirit fell among them (Acts 1:3 and 2:1-4).

Even Jesus had to wait patiently from the time He was twelve when He knew of His calling (Luke 2:42-50), until He finally began His ministry at age thirty (Luke 3:23). That's nearly twenty years of being tested and waiting for God to mature Him enough so He could bear the weight of the ministry without breaking under the pressure. Remember, "we do not have a High Priest who cannot sympathize with our weaknesses, but [Who] was in all points tempted as we are, yet without sin" (Hebrews 4:15).

When we walk through the valley of the shadow of death, we can rest in knowing that not only is our Heavenly Groom walking through this trial with us, but that He knows the way because He has already been through it. Jesus said, "In the world you will have tribulation; but be of good cheer, I have overcome the world" (John 16:33). When you experience rest during a trial, you are walking through the Promised Land (Joshua 21:44) and God is pouring out His grace to you.

Many people will never experience this paradise here on earth. Why? To live in this heavenly place, you must let go of your fears, let go of control and trust God to lead you when you don't see a way out of your trial. That means you must trust the Lord to be your spiritual eyes and ears, especially since He is the God of eternity and sees into the future while you can't.

Be thankful for the times when you trust your

Heavenly Father completely and reap the reward of joyfully walking through the Promised Land. Now, your next goal should be to dwell there continually, providing that you're willing to die to yourself daily. If you're prepared to make such a sacrifice, you'll find your haven of rest (Psalm 91).

Has God given you a promise or a vision? Don't lose hope! The Lord uses these "silent years" to perfect us in patience and faith so we'll be mature enough to fulfill His call on our lives. What happens to us next can be defined by our current response to the trial we're in! God wants us to use adversity as a steppingstone to bring us into a whole new realm of His restful presence while tribulation reveals exactly where we are spiritually at that moment.

What we need to remember is that "the bigger the problem we face, and the stronger the enemy that comes against us, the more mighty and majestic God will be… for us, and the greater the revelation of Himself He'll be able to give us." [27] Keep pressing on until you find God, no matter what's happening around you. Then, you will walk in victory.

Even if, like Joseph, your overwhelming conditions take you in what seems to be the completely opposite direction of what God has revealed to you, He has everything under control! When you keep your eyes focused on the Lord and patiently persevere by holding onto His promises, then He, Himself, will bear your sorrows. Then, one day, perhaps when you least expect it, you'll suddenly find that you're no longer forgotten in prison. Instead, you'll be elevated to a position of authority in the King's own house and find yourself in the Promised Land. Psalm 34:15, 17, 19, 22 declares,

> The eyes of the Lord are on the righteous, and His ears are open to their cry...The righteous cry out, and the Lord hears, and delivers them out of all their troubles...Many are the afflictions of the righteous, but the Lord delivers him out of them all...The Lord redeems the soul of His servants, and none of those who trust in Him shall be condemned. [Emphasis author's]

"SURELY HE BORE OUR SORROWS"

Do not grow weary in waiting on your Redeemer
While patience is developed in the heartland
   of your soul.
Trials strengthen the lives of Spirit-filled
   believers
Who lean on their Creator and sever fleshly
   control.

A higher level of faith is the essence of your
   training
When adversity strikes while you're engaged
   in heavy warfare.
As peace abounds within you, know you're
   steadily gaining
Stolen ground from the enemy as you trust
   God with your cares.

Are you fearful or angry when trials knock at
   your door?
Do you despair when, instead, you should rise
   and take action
Against evil forces that want to crush you in
   this war?
Be on guard; don't give in to a fleshly
   reaction!

Die to your flesh, child, and don't be misled
By thoughts and feelings that exalt themselves
   above the Lord.
Respond in the Spirit, not through your head;
Satan will flee when you wield God's
   powerful Sword.

Do not blame the Lord or others when He
   requires you to grow.
When you pass through troubled waters He'll
   be with you;
When you walk through the fire you'll not

be burned by your foes!
Jesus knows your predicament: He's already
  walked in your shoes.

Job was afflicted, yet remained righteous in
  God's sight.
Joseph was imprisoned, but persevered 'til the
  Lord promoted him.
These men held fast to their integrity and did
  what was right:
Will you, too, be found faithful when the light
  appears so dim?

Jesus knows your hurts, for He wept over
  Mary and Martha's pain,
And Lazarus, until He raised him from the
  dead.
Because He was mocked, mistreated, rejected,
  and disdained
Jesus knows your suffering through the tears
  that He's shed.

Can you see Him walk on the water when
  you're on the rough sea?
Do you find rest when the weather attempts to
  capsize your boat?
Deliverance will come when you seek Him on
  your knees
God's presence will help you to thrive and not
  just cope.

Many are the afflictions of God's righteous
  saints,
But the Lord is faithful to deliver them out of
  them all.
Those who wait upon the Lord shall be
  renewed and not faint!
Listen when He says, "Trust Me" and obey
  Him when He calls.

Jesus, our Deliverer, was despised, and we
  esteemed Him not;

A Man of pain, acquainted with grief, He
    holds our tomorrows.
He's our Savior, Healer, and with His own
    blood we've been bought.
Jesus knows our affliction, for surely He bore
    our sorrows.

CHAPTER FIVE

"...AND BY HIS STRIPES WE ARE HEALED"

"Surely He has borne our griefs and carried our sorrows; yet we
esteemed Him stricken, smitten by God, and afflicted.
But He was wounded for our transgressions, He
was bruised for our iniquities; the chastisement
for our peace was upon Him, <u>and by
His stripes we are healed</u>."
[Emphasis author's]
(Isaiah 53:4-5)

     While we wait for God's answer to our hearts' deepest
cries, the silence can sometimes be excruciating, especially
when our world rages against us like an angry sea. The
delay can be agonizing; the frustration can be overwhelming,
especially if our prayers are for physical health or restoration
of a relationship. If we allow Satan to negatively alter our
thinking, our faith in the Lord's goodness and love toward us
can shrivel up like a dry, empty husk.

     We need to guard our hearts from evil influence so the
bitterness and anger toward God which we wrongly carried
from our life experiences don't threaten to resurface with a
vengeance. If we allow these evils to grow roots in us (instead
of rooting them out), they'll grow like wild weeds until they
choke out all peace and joy in us. Proverbs 4:23 gives this
warning, "Keep your heart with all diligence, for out of it spring
the issues of life."

     We can't afford to have a polluted well because it will
clog our communication with God. Jesus said in Matthew 5:8,
"Blessed are the pure in heart, for they shall see God." Seeking
momentary, worldly pleasures is too high a price to pay when it
means sacrificing a close relationship with the Lord. John 4:23
reveals Jesus' heart, "...the true worshipers will worship the
Father in spirit and truth..."

DOES GOD REQUIRE THAT WE "HAVE FAITH" TO BE HEALED?

Sometimes, in the midst of this waiting time of prayer, satanic attacks come fast and furious. They may even come from our own Christian brothers and sisters. Statements such as "if the Lord isn't answering you, you must be hiding secret sin" may seem innocuous enough, but in reality, they are subtle attacks aimed at undermining our relationship with God and making us feel insecure or fearful.

Though the first statement may be true in some situations, it doesn't necessarily have to be. If a person has a clean heart and conscience before the Lord, such a statement from a well-meaning brother or sister in Christ may only cause the person to doubt whether or not his sins are really forgiven (to fully understand how much damage this can do to a believer, read the book of Job). As for those doubters who would tell you, "Maybe this is God's will," don't internalize their words of doubt or unbelief, especially when the Lord has instructed you to hold fast to your confession of faith.

Smith Wigglesworth was an anointed and mighty healing evangelist who lived from 1859-1947. He was often referred to as "The Apostle of Faith" because he was one of the pioneers of the Pentecostal revival. He addresses the issue of healing in his book, *Ever Increasing Faith*.

> Disease is not caused by righteousness, but by sin. There is healing through the blood of Christ, and deliverance for every captive. God never intended His children to live in misery because of some affliction that comes directly from the devil. A perfect atonement was made at Calvary. I believe that Jesus bore my sins and I am free from them all. I am justified from all things if I dare believe. He, Himself, took our infirmities and [bore] our sicknesses; and if I dare believe, I can be healed. [28]

So, does God require that we "have faith" to be healed? Yes and no. While it's true that Jesus declared to several individuals, "your faith has made you well" in

Matthew 9:22, He also raised at least three people from the dead: Lazarus, Jairus' daughter, and the widow of Nain's son (John 11:1-44, Mark 5:21-43, Luke 7:11-17) and I believe we can all agree that a dead body has no faith at all. However, it must also be noted that a corpse has absolutely no doubt or unbelief either!

The man who asked Jesus to heal his demon-possessed son was lacking in faith when the Lord said to him, "...all things are possible to him who believes." (Mark 9:23). The man replied in verse twenty-four with "Lord, I believe; help my unbelief!" He realized he could not believe for his son's healing on his own strength because he understood his natural, human faith was not enough. This is why he asked Jesus to help him where he was weak in his carnal nature.

I find it interesting that Jesus didn't reprove this man for not having enough faith. After all, He had rebuked His disciples on more than one occasion for the same thing. So, why didn't He hold this man to the same standard that He did the twelve? The answer is found in Luke 12:47-48 in the parable of the faithful and evil servant:

> And that servant who knew his master's will,
> and did not prepare himself or do according to
> his will, shall be beaten with many stripes. But
> he who did not know, yet committed things
> deserving of stripes, shall be beaten with few.
> For everyone to whom much is given, from him
> much will be required; and to whom much has
> been committed, of him they will ask the more.

When we are "babes in Christ," the Lord is gracious to us and will sometimes give us blessings that we don't have the faith to contend for on our own (1 Peter 2:2). Often, He'll use the faith of another, such as a pastor, a healing evangelist, or a more mature brother or sister in Christ, to help "secure" our answer to prayer for us. However, as we "grow up" in our faith and exercise it regularly, He'll make us "work" harder for the things that used to come easily.

That may seem strange until we realize we do the same thing with our children. When they're small, we buy clothes and toys for them simply because they ask and because we love them. But as they mature, we start to teach them about the value of a hard-earned dollar and delayed gratification, primarily because we want them to mature.

It takes time and self-discipline to be in the presence of the Lord to grow in our faith. The man in the scene above had not spent the time around Jesus that the disciples had, so little was required of him. Yet, for all the many months the twelve had been with Jesus day and night, for all the times they'd seen Him cast out demons, and for all the times they themselves had previously done so, they still had not embraced the spiritual disciplines of prayer and fasting. There are no shortcuts when it comes to faith and discipline and perhaps that's why Jesus corrected them so firmly.

So, does the Lord require that we have faith in order to be healed? God is sovereign. <u>He does not</u> <u>depend upon</u> <u>our faith in order to heal</u>: <u>He has that ability whether we</u> <u>believe He does or not</u>. In 2 Timothy 2:13, the Apostle Paul reminds us, "If we are faithless, He remains faithful; He cannot deny Himself." However, He needs us to be His hands and feet on this earth to bring hope and healing to those who are still in darkness. He cannot use us as effectively if we remain in doubt and unbelief or if we grow spiritually lazy and rely on someone else's anointing!

Someone must have the faith to usher in God's kingdom here on this earth. If you are born-again, the Lord has ordained and commissioned you to do just that! But first, you must exercise and grow in your faith so that you— yes, you—can do even greater works than Jesus did when He was here in the flesh. He declared in John 14:12, "… he who believes in Me, the works that I do he will do also; and greater works than these he will do, because I go to My Father."

I firmly believe it isn't God's will for us to be captives to pain and sickness. If anything, these afflictions should be afraid of us because Jesus already conquered them on the cross. But there still remains the nagging question, "Why, then, does the Lord heal some and not others?"

WHEN GOD DOESN'T HEAL

We know from Paul's second epistle to the Corinthians that there are circumstances when God chooses to not heal a believer. Paul talks about the "thorn in the flesh" that was sent to him in 2 Corinthians 12:6-8. *Halley's Bible Handbook* indicates that many commentators agree that his "thorn," which Paul calls a "messenger of Satan," refers to chronic ophthalmia, a condition which causes incredibly bad eyesight. [29]

Paul needed to dictate his letters to Tertius, his scribe (Romans 16:22), and would sign a brief passage at the end to show the letter's authenticity. In Galatians 6:11, he writes, "see with what large letters I have written to you with my own hand," and in 2 Thessalonians 3:17, Paul states that his signature is "with [his] own hand, which is a sign in every epistle; so I write."

No doubt, Paul's poor vision posed a great deal of problems on his many missionary journeys and made his profession of tent-maker even more difficult. Imagine how helpless he must have felt for always needing someone to guide him through strange towns and of constantly requiring help even to write letters. His eyesight became so bad that when he was brought before the Jewish council for preaching the Gospel (Acts 23:1-5) he was unable to recognize the High Priest, from whom he had personally received letters to put Christians to death (Acts 9:1-2), and who was easily recognizable by his garments, if nothing else (see Exodus 39). How humbling!

On top of all this, chronic ophthalmia causes severe inflammation of the tissues of the eyes, which results in facial disfigurement. [30] Paul notes the compassion of the Galatians in that they "would have plucked out [their] own eyes and given them" to him (Galatians 4:15). No wonder he "pleaded with the Lord three times that it might depart" in 2 Corinthians 12:8.

However, God knew what was best for Paul and his ministry. Through this physical trial, this faithful servant learned to lean wholly on God's grace and not on his own natural talents and strength.

As a result, Paul was able to say "most gladly I will rather boast in my infirmities, that the power of Christ may rest upon me...I take pleasure in infirmities, in reproaches, in needs, in persecutions, in distresses, for Christ's sake. For when I am weak, then I am strong" (2 Corinthians 12:9-10).

Rather than giving in to the fear of not being able to carry
on with his ministry because of his visual impairment, Paul
allowed God's love to mature him and to teach him how to
lean on the Lord for the strength to continue.

His faith was unshakable; he knew the promises of
God and he also knew His power firsthand. If being the
center of riots, mobs and stonings did not quench the strength
of his trust in the Lord's provision, then surely he could
believe the Holy Spirit was able to heal him. The Lord even
used him to heal many others, but why wasn't he restored?
The answer is found in the second part of verse seven. This
infirmity was God's grace to keep him from being "exalted
above measure," so he wouldn't become too proud about
all the visions and wondrous works the Lord was revealing
through him.

Please note that unless you're having an abundance of
revelations (2 Corinthians 12:7), and unless God is working
"unusual miracles" through you (Acts 19:11-12), then you
shouldn't accept a "thorn in the flesh" as the Lord's will for
your life. Of course, if the Lord reveals to you that you must
live with an infirmity that plagues you, He'll give you the
grace to persevere through it.

In Paul's case, he clearly stated that it was "a
messenger of Satan to buffet" him (2 Corinthians 12:7).
If you're still convinced your ailment is from your Heavenly
Father, let me ask you this question: when was the last time
an entire city tried to worship you as a god? It happened to
Paul, not just once, but twice! (Acts 14:11 and 28:6).

For many of us, though, three factors will frequently
determine whether or not we'll be able to receive the healing
which has already been purchased for us at Calvary: if we
are quick to repent, quick to forgive, and quick to believe,
then we shall be healed. [31] Conversely, blatant sin and
disobedience to God will cause our prayers to go unanswered,
as will bitterness, unforgiveness and unresolved anger toward
others. Ignorance or outright unbelief of God's Word will
also keep us shackled in pain and sickness. Nothing will get
us out of the Lord's will and into Satan's hands faster than if
we are slow to repent, slow to forgive, and slow to believe the
promises of the Holy Bible.

At the same time, be aware that there are times when the Lord does not heal us. I recently joined a healing and deliverance evangelist-friend of mine, Fernando Perez, for several months in praying for a nine-year old boy who was diagnosed with terminal cancer and full of faith. He truly believed his Heavenly Father revealed to him that he would rise from his bed of sickness. He made physical progress and was strengthened spiritually during our prayer times. He even described feeling a burning sensation throughout his body when my friend laid hands on him and prayed for deliverance from this crippling sickness time and time again.

Unfortunately, this brave boy eventually succumbed to this deadly disease. His dear mother, his family, Fernando and I stood in faith to the very end, until the Lord took him to Heaven. He was not in sin, was full of faith and loved Jesus with all his heart. Then, why did he die? I wish I knew. Some things we won't find out until we get to Heaven.

Since then, his father rededicated his life to Christ because of the courage that his son showed until his last breath. God was, clearly, glorified through this courageous, young warrior through his stubborn will to live, his positive attitude and unwavering faith, despite excruciating pain. His faith helped him to live longer than anyone else who has ever battled this type of cancer. I have never seen such courage in someone so young. He truly touched my life and I miss him dearly. His witness for the Lord gave me a greater resolve to serve God with all my heart and to help as many people as possible who are hurting emotionally or physically.

Often, when a crisis is beyond our human understanding, God allows tragedy to strike so His good works can be revealed through us (John 9:3). This can include our spiritual growth, teaching younger believers how to grow in their faith, being used as a vessel to bring healing to others and increased compassion for hurting and spiritually lost people. So, even after our lives have ended here on earth, our memory and witness for the Lord will live on as an inspiration to others. This brings glory to God.

If this young boy were here today, I know he would encourage anyone who is still trusting God for their healing, despite years of prayer, to hold fast to their confession of faith. I, too, want to encourage you to persevere in your prayers for divine healing where you truly believe God is going to touch you miraculously. Only the Lord knows when your healing will fully manifest, so you must continue to contend for your health until your breakthrough transpires.

I've been wearing corrective lenses for near-sightedness and double vision symptoms since my childhood, yet I'm still trusting the Lord for my healing because He hasn't released me from believing for His divine touch on my optic nerve. Granted, God sometimes restores us through alternative ways such as surgical procedures, but vision specialists have told me that my condition can't be corrected through these means. So, I continue to trust God to touch me supernaturally.

Should the Lord reveal to me along the way that I qualify for having my eyesight completely restored through a new visual technology, I will pursue that avenue. But if that doesn't happen, I will continue to trust God for His divine touch over my visual impairment. If I don't live to see the day when my vision is completely restored, I will still serve the Lord with gladness and know He will give me the grace to endure because His love sustains us in all things.

When someone does not receive his healing, this should not be cause for anyone to judge that individual. This person may have a pure heart, no hidden sin, be full of faith, and abiding in the Lord without understanding why he hasn't been healed yet. This individual is to be commended for his perseverance, strong faith and may even have a greater testimony than a healed person because his loving, joyful, humble spirit is not dependent on whether or not his prayer for healing is answered. His walk with the Lord is unwavering because God's love sustains Him in the best and worst of times. Jesus is very pleased when He sees this kind of faith.

Allow your Heavenly Father to help you endure in sickness and in health, in good and tough times because it truly shows the genuineness of your heart and the depth of your love for Jesus. If you're trusting God for your healing and still waiting for its physical manifestation, despite years of tarrying, I commend you for your perseverance. Keep in mind that while you wait for your answer through prayer, that nothing compares with the deeper spiritual intimacy that you develop while you spend special time with the Lord.

At the same time, I must caution you to exercise wisdom. Some people have died because they refused medical treatment that could have helped them. They claimed their healing had to be divine and that they didn't need a doctor. Sometimes, this is the case and God performs a miracle. However, the Lord's hand does move through physicians and other health professionals, so make sure you consult with them when you're in need of medical attention. Otherwise, the result could be deadly.

GOD OPPOSES THE PROUD

Our Heavenly Father has made provision to heal us in every aspect of our beings, not just physically! But God desires something even more than our health: <u>He desires our love</u>, which requires that we humble ourselves and admit that we need Him. I've often wondered why He would require us to pray and wait for His response when He knows all of our needs already. Since He anticipates our requests, why, then, doesn't He just answer them ahead of time? For us to just acknowledge our needs and admit we don't have the resources to meet them requires that we humble ourselves when we ask God for help.

Why is humility important in His eyes? Pride is the original sin; it was pride that brought about Satan's downfall when he decided he wanted to "be like the Most High" and declared, "I will exalt my throne above the stars of God!" (Isaiah 14:12-14). Satan (then known as Lucifer) rebelled against the Lord Who had created him and, in his rebellion, took a third of the angels of Heaven with him, who became his demonic host as a result (Revelation 12:4).

But Satan didn't stop there. His hatred and jealousy of God led him to trap the first fruits of His earthly creation with the same sin. He persuaded Eve that if she ate of the forbidden fruit she would "be like God" (Genesis 3:5). I cannot imagine the depths of pain the Lord must have felt to have been thus betrayed twice! The glories of His creation—Lucifer in the spirit realm and Adam and Eve in the physical—all gave in to pride and, in so doing, rebelled against their Maker.

This is why the Lord hates pride so much! "God resists [sets Himself against] the proud, but gives grace to the humble" (James 4:6). No wonder our Heavenly Father sometimes uses our infirmities and hurts to expose our own helplessness! He wants to draw our attention back to our only source of healing: Himself. This requires that we humble ourselves and ask Him to help us, which must sound like beautiful music to His ears because He longs to commune with us.

The sin of pride is so deceitful that it has even crept into the Christian Church in some places when people take the doctrine of standing in faith to the "name-it-and-claim-it" extreme. This is nothing more than a thinly-veiled attempt to manipulate God and force His hand into action by the "power" of <u>our</u> words. Any avenue by which we strive to take the control of our lives away from the Lord is nothing more than idolatry!

If we picture ourselves healed or claim it often enough, that in and of itself will not make it so. There is nothing wrong with claiming the promises of God, which we find in the Holy Scriptures, or with visualizing our healing (because God wants us to see ourselves healed) as long as we realize we cannot use those things to control the Lord. When we trust Him for our restored health, we must be certain we are led by the Holy Spirit and stand on His promises through the Word of God.

There is a very thin line here between faith, which is rooted in <u>the power of God's Word</u>, and witchcraft, in which people use the power of <u>their</u> words and positive mental images to alter circumstances based on their own strength. Therefore, when it comes to believing or "standing on" the promises of God, the bottom line is this: do you do so out of humility and submission to the Lord, <u>no matter what the outcome</u>, or do you believe because of your positive mental attitude that your words will force Him into action? He will heal us in His time and according to His divine plan. A completely surrendered believer relinquishes control to God.

Please don't misunderstand me. Our Heavenly Father wants us to have a positive attitude that's developed and refined by leaning on the Holy Spirit for strength through our trials. His ability to answer our prayers, though, is not dependent solely on our attitude, especially a fleshly one! David Wilkerson, the founding pastor of New York City's Times Square Church and a renowned, Christian evangelist, comments:

> The Church's concept of faith has been corrupted by our American culture. People in this country have been feeding on a demonic gospel of self-esteem, self-worth, self-help. We've been told, "believe in yourself." Then add that to our obsession with "instant everything"—instant meals, instant drinks, instant information, instant gratification...This has produced a temporary, false faith. People today are running to God's altar with no real conviction...they don't have true faith. What they have is presumption. [32]

Often, when we pluck a scripture for healing out of its context, we fail to see that there may be character or repentance requirements to be met before the healing can happen. No amount of visualization or meaningless, repetitious prayers, which Jesus warned us about in Matthew 6:7 will change that. Exodus 15:26 reminds us, "If you diligently heed the voice of the Lord your God and do what is right in His sight, [and] give ear to His commandments and keep all His statutes, [then] I will put none of the diseases on you which I have brought on the Egyptians. For I am the Lord who heals you" [emphasis author's].

Psalm 37:5 also says, "Commit your way to the Lord, trust also in Him, and He shall bring it to pass" [emphasis author's]. Trust is birthed through our love relationship with Jesus. On the other hand, doubt, fear and unbelief are conceived through the father of all lies: Satan, himself. Faith is stronger than fear by far, though the enemy of our souls would like us to believe otherwise.

"BUT GOD GIVES GRACE TO THE HUMBLE"

In 2 Chronicles 7:14, God immediately captures our attention, "if My people who are called by My name will humble themselves, and pray and seek My face, and turn from their wicked ways, then I will hear from heaven, and will forgive their sin and heal their land." According to this verse, there are several ways—humility, prayer, seeking God's face, and turning from our wicked ways—which the Lord uses as a means to facilitate healing in our lives. We would be wise to heed His call to repentance, especially since He's always looking out for our best interests.

HUMBLING OURSELVES THROUGH PRAYER

Prayer, when coupled with studying God's Word, acts as a life-preserver to keep us afloat when the waves of adversity threaten to drown us. How? By humbling ourselves before God as we surrender our fears and make our requests known to Him, we show Christ the depth of our love and commitment by waiting patiently for Him to answer us.

Often, we miss out on the best part of prayer by merely verbalizing a long list of our needs before we rush out to meet all the demands of the day. This is not humility; it's like telling a waiter what you want and expecting him to bring it immediately. Then, we wonder why the Lord doesn't speak to us the same way He speaks to others.

When we make the sacrifice of pushing away thoughts of accomplishing everything on our to-do list and choose instead to spend special time praising and listening to the Holy Spirit, He is greatly pleased with us and we're able to hear His voice more clearly. That is not to say we can't ask God for things we need—we still can—but we should balance our petitions to the Lord with worship and being still so we can hear His voice and instructions.

Prayer is the key to unlocking the promises that God has for us. If we can find scriptures which promise us those things for which we ask, we can have the confidence of

knowing we are in His will. Then, we can pray the prayer
of faith, believing that He will answer us and we can thank
Him thereafter for the answer, whether it comes immediately
or later. He delights in His Bride asking Him for help and
He takes pleasure in lavishing gifts upon us because of the
tremendous amount of love that He has for us. 1 John 5:14-
15 declares:

> Now this is the confidence that we
> have in Him, that if we ask anything according
> to His will [His promises in His Word], He
> hears us. And if we know that He hears us,
> whatever we ask, we know that we have the
> petitions that we have asked of Him.

And again, Mark 11:22-24 says,

> Have faith in God. For assuredly, I say to
> you, whoever...does not doubt in his heart, but
> believes that those things he says will be done,
> he will have whatever he says. Therefore I
> say to you, whatever things you ask when you
> pray, believe that you receive them, and you
> will have them. [Emphasis author's]

RACHEL'S HEALING

Several members of my own family have experienced
the Lord's miraculous touch firsthand. When my daughter,
Rachel, was twelve months old, I dropped her from my
shoulders onto the kitchen floor and she landed on the left
side of her head. I lost her when my oldest son, Joshua, (age
two and a half at the time) was climbing the counter and
began to fall.

As I attempted to catch him, I panicked. I lost my
firm grip on my baby girl, who was resting right above
me. Her fall was so shocking and painful that she cried
uncontrollably for at least thirty minutes. I was completely
responsible for the suffering that she was now experiencing.

Her mother rushed her to a hospital where the doctor

who treated her found nothing immediately wrong. But in the weeks that followed, she noticed Rachel had stopped learning how to talk and she began having difficulty walking more than a few steps. By age two, she had finally stopped falling and colliding into walls, but she still couldn't run or jump. She also did not respond well to noises behind her and her vocabulary was limited to approximately thirty words, most of which were grossly distorted (the normal range for two-year olds is around 300 words).

Her mom finally convinced Rachel's doctor that she needed to be tested. The results revealed her left eardrum was very stiff and not vibrating properly, which caused severe distortion of the sounds that she could hear, and pointed to damage in the middle ear (which would have caused her to lose her balance). An MRI and EEG were ordered to discover the level of damage that had occurred to her brain and inner ear, as well as a full battery of hearing tests.

When the results were shared with us, I was devastated to learn Rachel had indeed suffered a hearing impairment (which had caused her to regress in her speech) and that it was more than likely the result of the fall from my shoulders. I felt totally helpless and was devastated! I felt guilty because she was suffering because of my poor judgment. I sought the Lord in prayer and repented of carelessness. I realized I should have been more cautious with Rachel. I should have been holding her hands tightly and watching over her with tender loving care. I felt the weight of the world on my shoulders and made no excuses.

I couldn't help but reflect on a story that my dad shared with me years ago when he was also holding two of his four children, one baby in each arm. Suddenly, something startled him and he began to lose one of his babies. As he tried to save one, the other began to slip from his hands. In the process, my dad dropped both babies! He said that my mom, who witnessed the event, was so upset with him that she asked him out of sheer frustration, "Couldn't you have at least caught one of them?" Needless to say, it took her a long time before she was able to trust him again to care for her children.

I wondered, "Wow! Is this a curse that runs in

the family that still needs to be broken?" But I quickly dispelled that theory because I wasn't about to blame my own carelessness on a generational curse. As I was crying out to the Lord in prayer concerning this crisis, and more importantly, the damage that I had caused to my daughter, the Holy Spirit comforted me by telling me that He was going to right this terrible wrong and miraculously heal my precious, little girl. I believed with all of my heart that God would fulfill this promise as a testimony of His healing power.

I felt prompted by the Lord to call my good friend and healing evangelist, Ed LaRose, to ask him to pray with us. Ed and I were friends for nearly thirty years and he is in Heaven now. He traveled to fifty countries while carrying a six-foot cross as a visual aid to remind people about the love of God and that Jesus died for their sins. The Lord worked many amazing miracles through this mighty man of God and he led more than one million people to salvation.

After I informed Ed of Rachel's accident, he unexpectedly showed up at our door two days later at 5:30 am. He had prayed over my daughter for an hour while doing a prayer walk in our neighborhood before he rang our door bell. Even though we had no immediate sign that she was healed (she was still asleep), we believed it was so. In fact, the Lord spoke to Ed during our prayer time and told him that Rachel was healed and when the doctor would check her again, he wouldn't find any traces of a hearing impairment whatsoever. After receiving this prophetic word from God through Ed, I thanked the Lord for healing her.

That same day, Rachel had more tests scheduled. Her hearing specialist found absolutely nothing wrong. She could hear a full range of sounds in both ears! Even Rachel's personality changed. She became much more loving and gentle and stopped having what seemed like constant temper tantrums. Because she could finally understand and communicate, her frustration left her and her vocabulary took off like a rocket and hasn't slowed down since.

We serve a God of miracles; don't ever allow anyone to tell you otherwise. Prayer and faith in God's healing power proved to be the keys that unlocked the Lord's promise to heal our daughter. Hebrews 11:6 declares; "without faith it is impossible to please Him, for he who comes to God must believe that He is, and that <u>He is a rewarder</u> <u>of those who</u> <u>diligently seek Him</u>" [emphasis author's].

If her mother and I had allowed the doctors' reports to persuade us to doubt; if we had turned to our own efforts "to do everything humanly possible" without humbling ourselves and pleading with the Lord on her behalf, would she be healed today? I honestly don't believe she would be. We needed to exercise our faith and seek God first for His healing plan, which we did, and He proved Himself faithful to us, like He always does.

For the next several years, Rachel would receive speech therapy to help her with articulation of words until her speech was restored to normal. Over time, she would flourish in school by consistently making honor roll, honor society and eventually receive "The President's Academic Award" for outstanding achievement. She is now a freshman at a major university and excelling in all her courses. She even made the Dean's Honor List in her first semester.

Thank you, Lord, for healing my precious daughter! Not only did I learn first-hand that God still performs miracles, but that He sometimes even covers us for our careless actions. Just don't make a habit of it because the Lord doesn't always rescue us from our poor decision-making. It's much better to be responsible.

JOSHUA AND JONATHAN'S HEALING

When my son, Joshua, was about ten years old, he came down with a very bad cough. As soon as I noticed, I began praying over him diligently. After several days, I noticed he wasn't getting any better. Shortly after, my best friend, Neal Kanzler, invited me to go with him to the Voice of Pentecost Church in San Francisco. It was a Thursday night and I knew if I went, I would not get much sleep that night, especially since I normally woke up around 4:30 AM to pray and get ready for work. But I sensed the Lord wanted me to go, so I told Neal that I would go with him to ask for prayer for my sick child.

It was a very enjoyable service and the praise and worship really ministered to me. At the end of the service, the healing evangelist invited people to come up to the altar for prayer for any needs that they had. I went up to the front to stand in proxy for my son.

When I shared my need with this evangelist, he asked me if I had a handkerchief. I told him that I didn't, but had a folded paper towel in my pocket. He replied, "That will do." He anointed the paper towel with holy oil and I joined him in praying for healing for my son. After we finished, the evangelist instructed me to put the folded paper towel over Joshua after returning home and to pray over him.

When I arrived home around 1:30 AM, I was very exhausted but determined to pray over Joshua before collapsing from weariness. I took the anointed paper towel from my pocket, gently placed it over my son's throat while he was sleeping, prayed over him, and trusted God to touch him miraculously. The next day, he was significantly better and the day after, the coughing symptoms completely disappeared. The Lord was faithful to heal my boy.

A couple of days later, my youngest son, Jonathan, age seven at the time, began suffering from the same symptoms that his big brother had. Thankfully, I still had the anointed paper towel and I quickly placed it over Jonathan's throat while he slept. I prayed fervently over my child, believing that God would also touch him miraculously. Just like Joshua, Jonathan greatly improved the next day and the day after, the coughing symptoms miraculously disappeared. Thank You, Jesus! God was faithful to heal my two sons.

Afterwards, the Lord led me to read Acts19:11-12. It read, "Now God worked unusual miracles by the hands of Paul, so that even handkerchiefs or aprons were brought from his body to the sick, and the diseases left them and the evil spirits went out of them." The Holy Spirit revealed to me that I exercised the same healing practices as the apostle Paul and for my obedience in following the healing evangelist's instructions to pray over my children, God rewarded me by healing both of my sons.

Through this experience, I also learned that sometimes we have to make sacrifices and do something illogical in order for the Lord to move miraculously. In this case, I gave up badly-needed sleep so I could have an

opportunity to see my children healed. Granted, I went to work the next day very tired, but it was worth it and I would gladly do it again.

God confirmed to me that obedience and sacrifice are pleasing to Him, especially when it requires that we do something extraordinary because we serve an amazing God who deserves every ounce of our worship. Hebrews 11:6 reminds us that "...without faith it is impossible to please Him, for he who comes to God must believe that He is, and that He is a rewarder of those who diligently seek Him."

HUMBLING OURSELVES THROUGH PRAISE AND WORSHIP

Praise and worship is another avenue by which God moves through His people to facilitate the healing process. It is a way by which we may seek His face. Psalm 147:1-3 declares:

> "Praise the Lord! For <u>it is good to sing praises to our God</u>; for it is pleasant, and praise is beautiful. The Lord builds up Jerusalem; He gathers together the outcasts of Israel. <u>He heals the brokenhearted and binds up their wounds</u>" [emphasis author's].

The Lord delights in His children who come to worship Him in spirit and in truth. No matter how "untrained" your singing voice is, don't hold back your worship to let those with more talent do the praising for you. Wouldn't you think it strange if one of your children never talked to you or thanked you but allowed a sibling to do it for him or her? God wants to hear your thanksgiving and praise from your own lips!

I understand this concept in a very personal way: by the time my youngest son, Jonathan, was four, he still wasn't talking. Quite frankly, all the eloquent phrases my older children could verbalize at that point (as precious as they were) didn't bring me nearly as much joy as did the first "dada" spoken by my son, Jonathan, who had been silent for so long! This was music to my ears, especially since he was diagnosed with autism and verbal apraxia after he received a vaccination shot when he was fifteen months old.

He has progressed gradually since then and continues to improve as we wait patiently for the full, physical manifestation of His healing. I have prayed over him now for seventeen years and will continue to trust the Holy Spirit to guide me in my petitions for him as I trust God for the regeneration of his brain cells while Jonathan agrees with me through prayer and worship regarding his healing.

No matter how silly you think you may sound when you worship the Lord, your Heavenly Father delights in your efforts and is so proud of every baby step you take. Pastor Graham Cooke says he wouldn't be surprised if our "Proud Papa" tells the angel choir to quiet down just so He can hear you sing! [33]

Jesus declared that unless we "become as little children, [we] will by no means enter the kingdom of heaven" (Matthew 18:3). Many kids are not self-conscious; they aren't worried about what others might think of them or about how they'll measure up to someone else's expectations! Jesus continued in verse four, "Therefore whoever humbles himself as this little child is the greatest in the kingdom of heaven."

Psalm 8:2 reveals, "Out of the mouth of babes and infants You have <u>ordained strength</u>, because of Your enemies, that You may silence the enemy and the avenger." When Jesus quoted this verse in Matthew 21:16, He changed it to "You have <u>perfected praise</u>" [emphasis author's]. Did Jesus misquote the Scripture? Not at all. Rather, He had a fuller understanding of the Hebrew root words, "yasad" and "azaz." "Yasad" literally means "to establish, to lay the foundation, to instruct." [34] "Azaz" means "to prevail, to strengthen oneself, to be strong," and its conjugations are translated in various places also as "praise," "security," "majesty," "boldness," "might" and "power."[35]

Therefore, when we praise the Lord with the single-mindedness of a child, we strengthen and establish ourselves in the boldness and power of the Holy Spirit. We remove the focus from our own problems and instead fix our eyes on Jesus, in all His splendor and majesty. Psalm 22:3-5 declares,

"But You are holy, enthroned in the praises of Israel. Our fathers trusted in You; they trusted, and You delivered them. They cried to You, and were delivered; they trusted in You, and were not ashamed."

As we continue praising our Creator for what He has done, our hearts are led to worship Him for Who He is, drawing us into the very presence and glory of God. Fear must flee! Doubt must flee! Depression must flee! In God's Kingdom, we are called to live in righteousness, peace and joy in the Holy Ghost (Romans 14:17). As we exercise our faith in praising the Lord, our problems will pale in comparison to the incredible awesomeness of God!

In his book, *The Power Of Praise and Worship*, Terry Law describes how, through a friend, the Lord encouraged him to begin to praise and worship God following the sudden death of his wife. He describes having gone through a very sorrowful time following the loss of his life partner and how he struggled deeply in overcoming depression. Though it was very difficult for him at first because he was in deep mourning, he began to sing uplifting, spiritual songs.

He described how the enemy of his soul laughed at him in the beginning, trying to convince him that his praise was not genuine and that God had let him down because He did not save his wife from physical death. But Terry persevered by choosing to worship the Lord even though his despondent heart didn't feel like it. For his faithfulness, God broke the stronghold of depression over him and would later bless him with another beautiful, Christian wife.

HEALING THROUGH PRAISE AND WORSHIP

Psalm 40:1-3 also gives us an excellent illustration of how King David was strengthened as he placed his faith in God. It reads:

I waited patiently for the Lord; and He
inclined to me, and heard my cry. He also
brought me up out of a horrible pit, out of
the miry clay, and set my feet upon a rock,

and established my steps. <u>He has put a new
song in my mouth</u>—praise to our God; many
will see it and fear, and will trust in the Lord.
[Emphasis author's]

David's reward for waiting on the Lord was a song
from God that enabled him to praise Him in a new way. This
kind of worship is another weapon in our arsenal that will put
the enemy to flight and is, in fact, one of the highest forms of
praise! When we can still worship the Lord with all of our
heart from the depths of the pit of our Job-like circumstances,
we offer a much greater sacrifice than does someone who is
having a "mountaintop experience."
　　Job understood this when in Job 13:15 he said,
"Though He slay me, <u>yet</u> will I trust Him" [emphasis
author's]. When we can take our "thoughs," stare them
straight in the face, and still offer up a "yet," we will
have taken one giant step forward into maturity in Christ.
Habakkuk 3:17-19 gives us another example of this,

<u>Though</u> the fig tree may not blossom, nor fruit
be on the vines; <u>though</u> the labor of the olive
may fail, and the fields yield no food; <u>though</u>
the flock be cut off from the fold, and there be
no herd in the stalls—<u>yet</u> I will rejoice in the
Lord, I will joy in the God of my salvation.
The Lord God is my strength; He will make
my feet like deer's feet, and He will make me
walk on my high hills. [Emphasis author's]

A few years ago, the Lord showed me this principle
firsthand with a woman who came to me for counseling. Monica
had experienced tremendous abuse at the hands of her parents.
Rejection and unresolved anger became major themes in her life
and she suffered from ongoing depression because she refused
to forgive those who hurt her. As a result, she was unable to
develop any intimate relationships. Her lack of a strong support
system, as well as loneliness, conflicts with authority figures,
and a poor prayer life eventually led her to attempt suicide
repeatedly.
　　I met with her following a very severe, depressive

episode. She was in tears as she told me that she had lost total control of her emotions and a true reason for living. Of all the clients that I had ever met with, hers was the worst case of depression I had ever seen. <u>The Holy Spirit directed me to lead this very hurting woman in songs of praise and worship</u>. She was not able to join me initially because she was so overwhelmed with pain, but eventually, she did.

<u>After about fifteen minutes of singing to the Lord together, Jesus had completely broken Satan's stronghold</u> over her. Glory to God! She left the counseling session with a spirit of joy, victory, peace, and a complete absence of fear. She said she sensed God's love all around her and that He had given her new hope. A week later, she came to me in the same depressed state that she was in before. The Lord again directed me to praise and worship Him on behalf of this distraught woman. This time, after only five minutes of singing songs of adoration to the Lord, Satan's hold was broken off of her.

I had never before seen the Lord move in such a unique way in all my years as a helping professional. Only God could perform such a miraculous work! Remember: when we worship Him, the Holy Spirit shows up and will sometimes heal us when we praise Him out of the genuineness of our hearts.

As this example showed, praise and worship is not only an avenue through which we enter into God's presence, but is also a powerful tool to see Satan's strongholds broken over us, especially when we're in need of healing. As we are faithful to seek God's face, He will purify and heal the darkest corners of our hearts. <u>The Lord will turn what used to be a wasteland of hurt and heartache into an oasis filled with rivers of living water</u>.

HUMBLING OURSELVES BY OBEYING THE VOICE OF THE HOLY SPIRIT

Many times our healing is dependent upon our obedience to the voice of the Holy Spirit. Why is it so important to be in tune to His promptings? Because God is not limited to the time, place or manner in which He will move. He doesn't only speak at church altars or at healing services: He may choose to minister to us in our car, at a store, or in the middle of the night while we're in a deep asleep. We never know when God will open the door of opportunity and this is why we must be willing to follow His lead, no matter how strange or illogical that may seem. In the next two sections, I will share examples of how following the Holy Spirit's voice led to healing in my life.

EMOTIONAL HEALING FROM THE DEATH OF MY MOTHER

When I was seventeen and a senior in high school, my world was severely rocked when a nurse informed me that my mother, the person whom I loved more than anyone, only had a few hours to live since she was unexpectedly losing her battle to leukemia at the young age of thirty-six. Immediately after receiving this terrible news, I remember going into a bathroom, looking at a mirror, and saying, "This is all a dream. It's not really happening." I was afraid to face my emotional pain. I remained in this state of denial throughout the funeral and, to a large extent, for the next twelve years.

Each year when the anniversary of my mother's death approached, it would be increasingly difficult for me to contain my emotions. Because I had been taught it was not socially acceptable for men to cry (deception), I had denied a part of my humanity that was dying to express itself. God would eventually heal me in a very unique way.

On the twelfth anniversary of my mom's death (four years after I became a Christian), the Lord spoke to me very clearly in a quiet voice during my prayer time. He said, "I want you to go to San Francisco today and walk through the twelfth floor of the hospital where your mother died so I can heal you." Though I didn't even remember where it was, I drove by faith, believing that God would lead me so I could overcome this horrible tragedy.

However, as I was leaving Sacramento, one of the tires to my car blew out. I was unable to change the tire because the wind was so strong that it kept blowing my vehicle off the jack. So, I called my roommate, George Magallanes, and asked him to help me take my automobile to a tire shop where the problem could be taken care of. George was able to put a spare tire on my vehicle and we drove to a nearby automotive shop. He stayed with me as the day wore on. Shortly after, I realized I

would probably not make it to my destination.

Out of frustration, I silently prayed, "Oh Lord, I really don't want to go through this suffering for another year!" At that moment, George reminded me that his father had died two days earlier and was still struggling deeply with the loss of his dad. I had been so preoccupied with my own grief that I had completely overlooked his. Immediately, the Holy Spirit spoke to my heart. He said, "Be there for your friend today, for you know what it's like to lose a parent, and because you were willing to go to San Francisco, you are healed!"

Suddenly, I physically felt the Holy Spirit rip out the deep ache that had been lodged in my heart for so many years. The constant, gnawing, emotional pain I carried throughout my young adulthood was miraculously removed! Jesus wiped away in an instant the continual sorrow that surfaced whenever I thought about my mother as He spoke those freeing words of healing into my heart. I was and still am in awe that God could move in my life so quickly and yet, so delicately.

In the same manner in which He told Abraham to offer up his son, Isaac, as a sacrifice to Him for the testing of his faith (Genesis, chapter 22), He chose to heal me out of His tender grace and mercy as He looked at my willingness to do what He had commanded. The Lord removed my deep hurt and the fear of facing this tragedy through His amazing, bountiful love in much the same way in which He spared Abraham's son because of his willingness to obey the Lord because of his healthy fear (reverence) of Him (Genesis 22:11-14).

In the secular counseling theory and practicum courses I took while earning my Master's Degrees, I was taught that emotional healing cannot take place until the "counselee" has sufficiently worked through unresolved anger and grief. In my heart, though, I knew I had not accomplished those prerequisites and had more grief to work through when God chose to heal me miraculously. I even remember telling myself, "This is not supposed to happen this way!"

God revealed to me that I would never shed another sorrowful tear over my mom's death because He assured me that my healing was complete. He was right. I have shed tears of joy in reminiscing about happy memories of my beautiful mother having heart-to-heart talks with me and playing with me as a child, but never tears of anguish.

In the twinkling of an eye, God completely shattered the erroneous wisdom of man with three simple words, "You are healed!" Thirteen years later, the Lord quietly spoke to my spirit about the healing He accomplished concerning my mother's death. He said to me, "Man cannot put Me in a box. I am the Great Physician and I am sovereign. Beware of false teachings and mistaken ideas about Me so you don't allow them to get in the way of your healing."

PHYSICAL HEALING AT A CHURCH SERVICE

In the spring of 1995, my faith was tested again after I suffered an injury while playing in a softball game. I slid head-first into third base, landing on my left shoulder. Immediately, my shoulder felt tight and began to throb, so I knew I had injured it. Later, my doctor informed me that I had torn the tendons around my rotator cuff and the best he could offer me was medication for symptom relief and rest. I chose to not take medication and opted to rest my shoulder as much as possible. Unfortunately, I could tell my shoulder still hadn't improved after several months because each time I tried to do a military press (lifting a long bar with weights directly over my head), I would feel a sharp pain in the injured area.

After my last doctor visit, I made an appointment with my good friend and highly skilled massage therapist, Ladis Kapka, to see if he could help me. Shortly after, I heard that a well-known healing evangelist, Benny Hinn, was planning on holding a healing service in Sacramento. Once I confirmed through my church that he was indeed coming, I knew instantly in my heart that the Holy Spirit wanted me to attend this prayer meeting. So, I canceled my massage appointment because I truly believed the Lord would heal me supernaturally.

Toward the end of this healing service that I attended, this anointed minister led the gathering through a powerful time of praise and worship. After that, he had everyone lift up their prayer needs before the Lord where they were sitting or standing. As he prayed, I let my Heavenly Father know my motive for desiring to be healed, more than anything else, was so I could hold my babies, Joshua and Rachel, with both of my

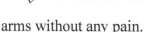

arms without any pain.

Then, this evangelist announced, "God is healing someone's shoulder up in the balcony right now," which is where I was standing. As soon as I heard this, I quietly said to God, "That's me, Lord!" Even though I didn't feel any physical sensations of warmth or tingling (like I've felt before when I've been healed miraculously from other injuries), I left trusting that the Holy Spirit had healed me.

When I arrived home at about 11:30 PM, I picked up my weights and did three sets of military presses for my shoulders with no pain for the first time in approximately four months. Hallelujah! The Lord was faithful to carry out the promise that He had spoken to me in my heart. The Holy Spirit miraculously healed me on this special night!

EXERCISING OUR FAITH

Romans 12:3 reminds us that "God has dealt to each one a measure of faith." It is up to us, though, to exercise our trust in Him. Otherwise, we're squandering the gift our Heavenly Father has given us. Every time we are faithful to obey the leading of the Holy Spirit, God will answer us and strengthen our faith.

The opposite is also true; each time we disobey God, we allow rebellion to creep in and our trust in Him is weakened, thus taking away the spiritual power we need to believe for healing for ourselves or for someone else. Then, when we really need it, the strength to believe in God's promises won't be there and we'll be easy prey for disillusionment, doubt and despair.

Does that mean God can't heal us when we're in a weakened, disobedient, spiritual state? Not at all! I know of instances where He has healed someone physically who had been living a rebellious life out of His grace and mercy. But it's much better to be in right standing with the Lord so we don't hinder our healing.

Sometimes, disobedience comes in the form of ignoring very practical advice. If, for example, you've been healed of lung cancer or emphysema and you continue to smoke; if you've been healed of digestive disorders and you revert to eating unhealthy foods; or if you've been healed of back problems and you keep lifting heavy objects incorrectly, then you are courting disaster. The medical profession possesses significant insight into how the human body functions best. We would be wise in listening to their recommendations.

But if we scornfully refuse to get rid of our bad habits, then we'll reap the evil fruit from the corrupt seed that we've sown. Sometimes, ignorance and poor decision-making are our worst enemies because they keep us from humbling ourselves before the Lord. God reminds us in Hosea 4:6: "My people are destroyed for lack of knowledge." We need to exercise wisdom by applying the knowledge we've been given so we can live pure, healthy, productive lives.

In both instances where I received emotional healing over my mom's death and physical healing over a torn rotator cuff, I could have just ignored the Holy Spirit's promptings or rationalized them away and stayed home. In that case, God would not have loved me any less and my salvation would not have been in jeopardy, but I would still be a very hurting individual, emotionally and physically, because of disobedience. Just as a bodybuilder grows stronger and more defined when he continues to lift weights regularly, our spiritual faith-muscles need to be exercised consistently through obedience to our Heavenly Father so we can grow in the Lord.

ONE SACRIFICE FOR ALL TIME

When Isaiah prophesied about the coming Messiah in the verses quoted at the beginning of this chapter— "by His stripes we are healed" (Isaiah 53:5)—he obviously spoke it before Jesus' death on the cross. But look at what Peter wrote, quoting from Isaiah after Jesus' atonement for us: "by whose stripes you were healed" (1 Peter 2:24). The Lord already bore the penalty of pain and sorrow because of our sins.

We know His part of the covenant is fulfilled because He declared in John 19:30, "It is finished!" Our part is not complete, however, until we exercise the faith to believe that our needs and the needs of our loved ones have already been met. We must simply accept the gift of healing that He has bestowed upon us that comes with releasing our fears and placing our trust in Christ.

If this sounds too simplistic to you, let me ask you this: how did you receive your salvation? And how did you receive

the baptism of the Holy Spirit? Were they not gifts freely given to you? There was nothing you could have done to earn them; you simply received them by faith, trusting that the Lord would perform what He had promised. Receiving our healing, whether emotional or physical, is no different.

We know our Heavenly Father desires to bless us. He distinctly declares this often in His Word (Genesis 22:17, Genesis 12:3, Hebrews 6:14). It is God's will for His Bride to receive healing over sicknesses, diseases, emotional pain, hurting relationships and spiritual struggles. He loves us and declares this to us as an everlasting covenant:

> You whom I have taken from the ends of the
> earth, and called from its farthest regions,
> and said to you, "You are My servant, I have
> chosen you and have not cast you away: Fear
> not, for I am with you; be not dismayed, for I
> am your God. I will strengthen you, yes, I will
> help you, I will uphold you with My righteous
> right hand." (Isaiah 41:9-10).

Why would we ever believe that God delights in seeing us suffer? If you find yourself questioning whether the Lord can do the same kinds of miracles today that we read about in the Bible (healing or other kinds of miraculous works), my answer to you is a resounding "Yes!" God does not change (Hebrews 13:8) nor has His power diminished since then. By failing to trust Him with our healing, we're saying that Jesus' sacrifice was only partial at best and that fear is stronger than the love of the One Who has betrothed us to Himself. Nothing could be further from the truth!

Let us boldly look beyond the physical realm and trust that we are healed, whether it happens instantaneously, progressively or in Heaven, should the Lord choose to call us home. Begin to thank God ahead of time for the answer, and continue to do so until you see the full manifestation of it (the Lord already sees it!).

I once heard a pastor share that God gave him an image of why people don't receive their healing. He showed him a weight scale where one side contained a person's prayers and the other side contained thankfulness to God for answered prayers.

The scale was tipped significantly to the side labeled: "petitions for prayer."

God pointed out to this minister that His people need to thank Him for their restoration ahead of time, even when they're still hurting and can't feel or see their healing fully manifest yet. Why? Because the Lord told him that this is an act of faith that will accelerate their restorative process and will more evenly balance the scale to the side that reads "thankfulness."

To illustrate, I've been a competitive, tournament-going arm wrestler for 28 years and the Lord has blessed me with 26 World Arm Wrestling Championships, 10 United States National Titles, 27 California State Championships and 129 career titles. I pursued this sport as a ministry to share with others where real strength comes from: Jesus! To prepare for an upcoming tournament, I was practicing with Joey Viera, another world champion and very skilled arm wrestling competitor. In the heat of the battle, I heard a popping sound come from Joey's elbow and we immediately stopped wrestling.

Joey had apparently pulled a tendon and was in severe pain. I quickly asked him if he would allow me to pray for him. He agreed and I prayed a prayer of faith, trusting that God would bring complete restoration to the injured area.

Afterwards, I was prompted by the Holy Spirit to tell my friend, "Joey, when you drive home today, I want you to thank the Lord for healing your arm, even if it still hurts." He agreed to do so. Two days later, he called and said, "Hey Victor, you're never going to believe what happened." I replied, "Try me." He continued, "I was driving home the other day after I was injured and I did what you told me to do—I thanked God for healing my elbow. As soon as I said that, the pain completely left me."

After hearing this good news, I rejoiced with Joey because our Heavenly Father blessed my friend for his obedience through my instructions as he spoke those things that were not as if they were (Romans 4:17). The Holy Spirit also reminded me what Jesus said in John 20:29: "...Blessed are those who have not seen and yet have believed."

Since I heard about this wonderful spiritual truth of thanking the Lord for our healing before we actually see it or feel it, God has also shown me that this is also an act of spiritual warfare. Why? Because we're declaring to the pain in our bodies and to Satan (since sickness and disease originate from him) that our faith supersedes our wounds.

We're making it known that no matter how much hurt we feel, our ailment and the enemy of our souls does not have any power over us. This is Job-like faith and the same faith that Shadrach, Meshach and Abednego (Daniel 3:16-28) exercised when they believed God would deliver them out of the fiery furnace, which He did!

Satan hates it when we declare to the heavenly realm that we'll continue to worship God, no matter what circumstances afflict us. I encourage you to practice this spiritual truth. I believe it will accelerate your healing. After all, looking at our circumstances through Heaven's perspective is what faith is really all about.

The choice is ours: will we love God and faithfully persevere or will we doubt Him and be bound by fear? Let us rest in God's promises and trust the Lord for our healing, for by Jesus' stripes, we are healed!

"BY HIS STRIPES WE ARE HEALED"

How do you respond when you're tossed to and fro
By rough seas that threaten to capsize your boat?
Do you seize the opportunity to blossom and grow
Or does your faith waiver when you struggle to stay afloat?

Many have gone before you who have suffered for the Lord.
They have faced death head-on with courage and hope
And have overcome despair as their faith was restored.
They, like you, know what it's like to be at the end of their rope.

You must know the promises and power of God firsthand.
Do not give in to doubt, unbelief or ignorance of the Word;
These will keep you shackled in pain and from the Promised
    Land.
Dare to trust the voice of Your Healer and the promises you've
    heard!

Humble yourself before the Lord and be quick to repent;
Forgive those who have hurt you so He can right all your
    wrongs.

God will purify your heart once you give Him consent
And in your hour of weakness, child, He will make you strong.

Seek godly counsel and be led by the Spirit of the Lord.
Obey the voice of your Shepherd; He'll help you face your pain.
Your daily walk with your Redeemer must not be ignored,
Lest you risk leaving this life emotionally maimed.

Do not exist in misery, heartache and despair.
Find the keys that unlock His promises through believing.
Remember that God will not give you more than you can bear.
So, be steadfast in your faith and trust God for your healing.

The prayer of faith will save the sick and the Lord will raise you
    up.
If you'll dare to trust Jesus, He'll help you with your unbelief;
If you know Him as your King, you're worthy to drink from His
    cup.
He will fill your desolate places and heal you of your grief.

Your barren wasteland of hurt and heartache will be replaced
By an oasis that flows from Heaven's throneroom of grace.
Filled with rivers of living water, they'll satisfy your taste;
A refuge of healing and restoration, behold your new dwelling
    place.

Jesus was wounded for our transgressions, bruised for our
    iniquities.
He bore the reproach for our peace and through the Spirit, He
    reveals
That His Presence is ever with us when we seek Him on our
    knees,
For we have hope through our Savior and by His stripes we are
    healed!

CHAPTER SIX

PERFECT LOVE CASTS OUT ALL FEAR

"Be strong and of good courage; do not be afraid,
nor be dismayed, for the Lord your God
is with you wherever you go"
(Joshua 1:9)

1 Corinthians 13:13 gives us the principles on which God's kingdom is founded, "And now abide faith, hope, love, these three; but the greatest of these is love." We also know that Satan perverts everything that the Lord made, therefore, his kingdom is founded on doubt, unbelief and fear and many other evils such as hatred and bitterness. Of these, the greatest is perhaps fear; for doubt and unbelief are spawned by fear just as surely as faith and hope spring forth from love. My question to you is this: on which foundation are you building your life?

Therefore whoever hears these sayings of Mine [Jesus], and does them, I will liken him to a wise man who built his house on the rock: and the rain descended, the floods came, and the winds blew and beat on that house; and it did not fall, for it was founded on the rock.

But everyone who hears these sayings of Mine, and does not do them, will be like a foolish man who built his house on the sand: and the rain descended, the floods came, and the winds blew and beat on that house; and it fell. And great was its fall. (Matthew 7:24-27)

Building on a foundation of fear will not only keep us from maturing in the Spirit, but it will also destroy our intimacy with Jesus. How can one realistically build anything of lasting value if the foundation is unstable? No matter how well-constructed the rest of the house may be its integrity will be compromised because it will have no firm undergirding to support it when the storms come.

If we are unable to step out in faith (unable to believe that not only does the Lord hear our prayers, but that He also answers them), then we'll never know the thrill of having our prayers answered and we'll never be able to fully rest in His promises. <u>Only in the comfort and security of God's love can we ever be completely at peace</u> because fear cannot enter where love is!

God never made us a promise He couldn't keep, nor has He ever asked anything of us which we could not do, <u>especially since we have His help</u>. So, what prevents us from being used by God to usher in the same kinds of healings and miracles today that were experienced in the Bible? After all, in John 14:12, Jesus said, "Most assuredly, I say to you, he who believes in Me, the works that I do he will do also; and greater works than these he will do, because I go to My Father."

I believe one reason we don't see the same number of mighty miracles is simply this: too many believers have built their lives on the wrong foundation by allowing fear, doubt, unbelief and deception to maintain strongholds in their lives. The Bride can have no depth of relationship with her Groom with such a brittle, spiritual house.

OBEDIENCE BRINGS VICTORY

Are you willing to take the step of faith that will propel you forward in the spiritual realm? Are you willing to sacrifice your fears for the security that's found in God as you choose to love our Heavenly Father by trusting Him? Are you willing to risk leaving the sins of your past and dare to enter the Promised Land where you'll find deliverance, hope and restoration?

The book of Exodus, chapters 7-15, tells us how the Lord delivered the Hebrew people from the slavery of Egypt. After the ten plagues and the Passover, Pharaoh finally decided to allow God's people to leave. On their way out of Egypt, God led the children of Israel through the wilderness toward the Red Sea. Then, to their surprise, Pharaoh's heart hardened yet again and he decided to pursue the Israelites with his men on chariots.

Exodus 14:10 records that, "when Pharaoh drew near, the children of Israel lifted their eyes, and...were very afraid..." Instead of trusting their Heavenly Father to finish what He started, the Hebrews complained to Moses about leading them to their deaths in the wilderness, declaring that they were better off as Egyptian slaves!

As a result, in Exodus 14:13-14, Moses spoke to the people and boldly proclaimed, "<u>Do not be afraid</u>. Stand still, and see the salvation of the Lord, which He will accomplish for you today. For the Egyptians whom you see today, you shall see again no more forever. The Lord will fight for you, and you shall hold your peace" [emphasis author's].

Because of Moses' faith, God instructed him, "Tell the children of Israel to go forward...lift up your rod, and stretch out your hand over the sea and divide it (verse 15). This fearless leader chose to put his faith in the Lord for deliverance no matter what the circumstances looked like and obeyed Him by walking forward into the sea.

He could see no way of escape with his natural eyes but as Moses obeyed by simply holding up his rod, God moved on their behalf. At times, the Lord will tell us to do something which seems totally illogical in the physical realm just to test our obedience or depth of love for Him. And it is often only <u>after</u> we obey the Holy Spirit's first command to us, that He'll open the way for us to proceed! Moses had to obey <u>before</u> the Red Sea could part, even though God's instructions made no sense at all.

David, as a young teenager, was required to take the very same step of faith the Hebrews did at the seashore. Valiant warriors who had likely proven themselves to be courageous in previous battles were not able to conquer fear and trust the Lord for deliverance because they grew afraid over what they saw: a mighty giant who towered over them (1 Samuel 17:4-11).

David, however, drew courage from remembering God's faithfulness when he helped him defend his flock from the lion and the bear (1 Samuel 17:34-37). David's faith and confidence in the Lord was so strong that when he faced Goliath in battle, not only did he wear no armor (1 Samuel 17:39), but 1 Samuel 17:48 reminds us that he "hurried and <u>ran toward</u> the army to meet the Philistine" [emphasis author's]. He didn't just stand there and wait for Goliath to come to him! Instead, he hurried to meet his enemy, fully trusting that God would give him the victory.

For us to learn from those who have gone before us, we must not forget that <u>these mighty men of God took a step of courage by moving forward in their faith when all seemed hopeless in the natural realm</u>. Whether our act of faith requires a single step or a giant leap, God loves us too much to not come through for us in our time of need.

FAITH IS A CHOICE

After being purified by the Lord in the wilderness for about two and a half years, the Hebrew nation stood for the first time on the border of Canaan, their Promised Land (Numbers, chapter 13). Then, God directed Moses to send out twelve men to bring back a report concerning the strength of their enemies, the fortifications of their cities and the natural resources of the land.

When they returned, they reported that the land was indeed fruitful—above and beyond what they expected, for two men were needed to carry just one cluster of grapes! However, ten of the spies brought back a report of doubt and unbelief. The people of the land were giants, and in comparison, the spies felt like mere grasshoppers (Numbers 13:33). In other words, they were afraid of what they had seen and didn't believe they were capable of possessing the land.

Pastor Edwin Louis Cole defines faith as "believing that what you cannot see will come to pass." [36] However, he also defines fear as "believing that what you cannot see will come to pass." [37] So, what's the difference? Notice his answer: "Faith attracts the positive. Fear attracts the negative." [38] In other words, those who choose to have a positive outlook, which is birthed in prayer, believe with all of their hearts that God will bring an answer to their dilemma. Those who have a negative attitude, on the other hand, do not truly believe the Lord will deliver them and even criticize Him while they fret over their plight.

Caleb and Joshua were the only two of the twelve who had a completely different perspective. After quieting the people who had begun to murmur against Moses, Caleb declared, "Let us go up at once and take possession, for we are well able to overcome it!" These two knew the Lord well enough to know that if He said the land was theirs, He would make good on that promise.

But the people refused to listen and chose to give in to fear. As a result of receiving this negative report, the Bible records that they became distraught and accused the Lord:

the congregation...cried, and the people wept
that night. And all the children of Israel
complained against Moses and Aaron, and the
whole congregation said to them, "If only we
had died in the land of Egypt! Or if only we
had died in this wilderness! Why has the Lord
brought us to this land to fall by the sword,
that our wives and children should become
victims? Would it not be better for us to return
to Egypt?" (Numbers 14:1-3)

The children of Israel were so bound by unbelief and
fear and became so agitated that they were ready to elect a
new leader who would take them back to Egypt, the land of
abuse and slavery from where they had just been freed. Then,
"Moses and Aaron fell on their faces before all the assembly of
the congregation of the children of Israel" (verse 5). I believe
this was out of shock and disbelief over the Israelites' rebellion
because Joshua and Caleb tore their clothes. The two of them
tried to encourage the people by reminding them of God's loving
promise to give them the land of Canaan:

The land we passed through to spy out is an
exceedingly good land. If the Lord delights
in us, then He will bring us into this land and
give it to us, a land which flows with milk and
honey. Only do not rebel against the Lord,
nor fear the people of the land, for they are
our bread; their protection has departed from
them, and the Lord is with us. Do not fear
them. (Numbers 14:7-9). [Emphasis author's]

Unfortunately, the Hebrews chose to believe the evil
report over the good one that Joshua and Caleb announced.
The Israelites were so discouraged that they lost their senses
and wanted to stone these godly men to death (verse 10).
Can you imagine? These people were ready to commit murder
because they allowed the news that was given to them by the
fearful spies to influence them to go astray. In other words, they
allowed negative peer pressure to rob them of God's peace and

complete trust in Him.

They began to rebel by doubting the Lord would deliver them from their enemies, which is the same as calling God a liar! In 1 Samuel 15:23, this mighty prophet reminds us that "...rebellion is as the sin of witchcraft..." Rebellion opens the door to the demonic realm and it cuts a person off from the Lord (Psalm 68:6). Since serving Christ is all about obeying Him while rebellion is the direct antithesis of what God desires from us, no wonder Samuel equates rebellion with witchcraft—its roots are intertwined with evil and we should have nothing to do with anything that attempts to draw us away from Jesus.

THE CONSEQUENCES OF UNBELIEF

God was now so disgusted with the Israelites' disloyal hearts that He was ready to kill them! Moses, however, pleaded for mercy and forgiveness. The Lord forgave His children for this sin, but not without consequences. Numbers 14:20-24 reveals His punishment:

> ...I have pardoned...but... because all these men who have seen My glory and the signs which I did in Egypt and in the wilderness, and have put Me to the test now these ten times, and have not heeded My voice...shall not see the land of which I swore to their fathers, nor shall any of those who rejected Me see it. But My servant, Caleb, because he has a different spirit in him and has followed Me fully, I will bring into the land where he went, and his descendants shall inherit it.

Later, God spoke to Moses and Aaron together concerning the sin of murmuring (criticizing), which the people of God committed. He announced to them,

> ...I have heard the complaints which the children of Israel make against Me. Say to them,...The carcasses of you who have complained against Me shall fall in this

wilderness, all of you...from twenty years old
and above. Except for Caleb...and Joshua...
you shall by no means enter the land which I
swore I would make you dwell in...And your
sons shall be shepherds in the wilderness forty
years, and bear the brunt of your infidelity,
until your carcasses are consumed in the
wilderness. According to the number of the
days in which you spied out the land, forty
days, for each day you shall bear your guilt
one year, namely forty years, and you shall
know My rejection. (verses 27-34)

God was infuriated! He was angry with His disobedient
children for not trusting Him to fulfill the promises that He had
guaranteed He would bring to pass. Their doubt and critical
spirit prevented them from ever dwelling in the Promised Land.
Their refusal to listen to the voice of the Lord through Joshua
and Caleb cost them the opportunity to experience an abundant
life.

Listen to the fate of the ten spies who brought back the
evil report, "the men whom Moses sent to spy out the land, who
returned and made all the congregation complain against him
by bringing a bad report of the land...died by the plague before
the Lord" (Numbers 14:36-37). God did not want those men to
infect His people with their negative, doubting spirits. If they
had repented and put their trust in the Lord, God might have
been merciful enough to lift this death sentence. But they were
not willing to humble themselves and the only way to ensure
the safety of the rest of God's people was to remove these evil
influences from among them.

Phillip Keller discusses this concept in his book, *A
Shepherd Looks At Psalm 23*. A shepherd himself, Phillip Keller
once owned a sheep that he loved very much.

She was one of the most attractive sheep that
ever belonged to me. Her body was beautifully
proportioned. She had a strong constitution
and an excellent coat of wool. Her head was
clean, alert, well set with bright eyes...But in

spite of all these attractive attributes she had one pronounced fault. She was restless—discontented—a fence crawler. [39]

He called her "Mrs. Gad-about" because she was constantly looking for ways to get around, under or through the fences of the pasture. Even though his fields were some of the best grazing grounds in the area, Mrs. Gad-about was not content to trust her shepherd but was apparently fearful that she might be missing something better elsewhere. Phillip Keller wasted many hours looking for her, and often when he had found her, it was evident she had ended up "feeding on bare, brown, burned-up pasturage of a most inferior sort." [40]

Soon, her lambs became just as rebellious as she was, and not long after that, she began to teach the other sheep of the flock to do the same.

After putting up with her perverseness for a summer, I finally came to the conclusion that to save the rest of the flock ...she would have to go. I could not allow one obstinate, discontented ewe to ruin the whole ranch operation. It was a difficult decision to make, for I loved her in the same way I loved the rest. Her strength and beauty and alertness were a delight to the eye. But one morning I took the killing knife in hand and butchered her. Her career of fence crawling was cut short. It was the only solution to the dilemma...It is a solemn warning to the carnal Christian—[the] backslider—the half-Christian—the one who wants the best of both worlds. Sometimes in short order they can be cut down. [41]

I wonder how many of us wander through deserts of our own choosing because we're afraid to trust our Shepherd? Even worse, how many of us will not live to see the fullness of our days because of our stubborn rebellion against our Maker? Notice that the ten spies were part of God's chosen people and the ewe that

disobeyed was one of the shepherd's favorites!

I'm not talking about non-believers here; these are examples of Christians who allow doubt, fear and unbelief to rule over them, thus leading other people of faith astray and causing Christ to be put to open shame (Hebrews 6:6). God is very loving, merciful, and patient with His children, but He will only give us so much time to repent and turn from our wicked, critical ways before He sends the destroyer to remove our evil influence from among His people (1 Corinthians 10:10).

THE BLESSINGS OF FAITH

Contrast the judgment which fell upon the ten fearful spies with the blessing given to the other two. Numbers 14:38 records that, "Joshua...and Caleb...remained alive, of the men who went to spy out the land." Their stand for God nearly cost them their lives since their own people wanted to kill them, but God delivered them and blessed them abundantly. Forty-five years later, when Joshua and Caleb had finished leading the people into the Promised Land, Caleb declared,

> And now, behold, the Lord has kept me alive, as He said, these forty-five years, ever since the Lord spoke this word to Moses while Israel wandered in the wilderness; and now, here I am this day, eighty-five years old. As yet I am as strong this day as on the day that Moses sent me; just as my strength was then, so now is my strength for war, both for going out and for coming in. (Joshua 14:10-11)

Not only had God kept the two of them alive, but He had also kept them in excellent health. After all, how many octogenarians do you know of who are capable of leading armies in hand-to-hand combat for five years straight? Though we don't know how old Caleb was when he died, we do know Joshua was one hundred and ten years old—still in full command of his mental faculties, and still a respected leader in Israel—when he went home to be with the Lord (Joshua 24:29).

CHOOSE THIS DAY WHOM YOU WILL SERVE

For those of us who have the vantage point of knowing how a historical event turned out, it's easy to criticize those who were caught up in the middle of what transpired. The Israelites' sin of doubting God's abilities may seem obvious to you, and you might ask, "How could they possibly doubt God after all the miracles that He performed to bring them out of Egypt?" And yet, as a result of condemning them, we become complacent about the very same issues which prevail in our own lives and we fall into the same trap of iniquity that the children of Israel succumbed to in the wilderness.

Linda had been divorced for ten years and even though she was a Christian and prayed desperately for a godly husband, she sabotaged relationship after relationship because she was afraid to trust. She had been hurt so many times in the past by men in her life that she was unwilling to allow the Lord into the intimate places of her heart. She didn't trust God either. How, then, could she really believe He would choose someone who was best for her?

One day, she took matters into her own hands and began dating an unbeliever at her work whom she had known for years, even though she knew the scriptural admonishment (2 Corinthians 6:14) against doing so. She rationalized, 'Well, at least he's emotionally stable, intelligent, financially secure, and has some Christ-like qualities." Quite frankly, she wanted to be in control. She wasn't willing to wait for God to heal her heart first. She ended up marrying this unbeliever and found out too late that there were many secret sins in his heart that she hadn't known about. Her marriage eventually ended in divorce because her impatience caused her to go her own way and marry outside of the will of God. She allowed her flesh to guide her rather than the Lord.

We see this same attitude in the Hebrews as they came out of their land of bondage. Four hundred and thirty years in the midst of an occultic nation had dulled their memories of Who God was and He had become just another deity to them (in line with all the Egyptian gods) who was too weak to deliver them from their yoke of slavery. Unfortunately, even though the

Lord showed Himself strong through all the miracles of their liberation, the Israelites still didn't trust Him on the other side of the Red Sea any more than they had in Egypt. Perhaps that's one reason why they built the golden calf (Exodus 32); that was something they could control.

DISOBEDIENCE BRINGS SHAME AND DEFEAT

If we choose to be independent of God, we lose His protection because we step outside of His will for our lives. As much as the Lord loves us, He will not force us to love and obey Him! When we walk away from Him, the comfort and security that comes with choosing to live for the Lord leaves us. Why? Because God cannot commune with rebellious spirits! There is no room for them in His kingdom.

The children of Israel found this out in a very graphic way during the battles with the cities of Jericho and Ai. Before the people went in to the Promised Land, the Lord had told Moses,

> You shall burn the carved images of their gods with fire; you shall not covet the silver or gold that is on them, nor take it for yourselves, lest you be snared by it; for it is an abomination to the Lord your God. <u>Nor shall you bring an abomination into your house, lest you be doomed to destruction like it.</u> You shall utterly detest it and utterly abhor it, for it is an accursed thing. (Deuteronomy 7: 25-26) [Emphasis author's]

Likewise, Joshua had specifically told the people in Joshua 6:18-19,

> And you, by all means abstain from the

accursed things, <u>lest you become accursed</u>
<u>when you take</u> of the accursed things, <u>and</u>
<u>make the camp of Israel a curse, and trouble</u>
<u>it</u>. But all the silver and gold, and vessels of
bronze and iron, are consecrated to the Lord;
they shall come into the treasury of the Lord.
[Emphasis author's]

The will of God in this matter was very clear; likewise,
the line between obedience and rebellion was obvious. Still,
after Jericho was miraculously defeated, one man, Achan,
despised the Word of the Lord and took things from the spoils of
the town which had been expressly forbidden in Joshua 7:21:
a "beautiful Babylonian garment," two hundred shekels of
silver, and a wedge of gold weighing fifty shekels." What was
the result? The Israelites were defeated and shamed at the battle
with Ai (Joshua 7:4-5).

Achan might have rationalized that the Lord wouldn't
really punish him for such a "little" transgression (minimizing),
and that he needed to "look out for number one" (selfishness),
besides being greedy. The unhealthy coping behaviors by which
we protect ourselves are no different! When we use them, we
proclaim to the heavenly realm that we don't trust the Lord to
heal us and care for us.

How can we think that God will just wink at our sin and
look the other way when we embrace "abominations" and hide
them just as Achan hid those things in his tent? In fact, God
did not take lightly what Achan had done. When Joshua came,
weeping and on his face before the Lord, to find out why they
had been defeated, God said to him in Joshua 7:10-12,

Get up! Why do you lie thus on your
face? Israel has sinned, and they have
also transgressed My covenant which I
commanded them. For they have even
taken some of the accursed things, and have
both stolen and deceived...<u>Therefore the</u>
<u>children of Israel could not stand before their</u>
<u>enemies</u>...<u>because they have become doomed</u>
<u>to destruction</u>. <u>Neither will</u> I be with you

anymore, <u>unless you destroy the accursed from among you</u>. [Emphasis author's]

Notice that Achan's sin, which was done in secret and hidden from all human eyes, impacted everyone around him. The Lord said, "Israel has sinned—not "Achan has sinned— and judgment was set against them all because of his personal rebellion. Don't forget that we are all one Body (Romans 12:4-5), and when one member is infected with sin, all the other members will suffer. Your personal sin and mine—weakens the Body of Christ like a deadly plague, so that, corporately, we cannot effectively stand before our enemies.

How did the Israelites sanctify themselves, remove the curse from their midst, and show the Lord that they wanted to love and serve Him? They took Achan and the things he had stolen, along with his children, his livestock and even his tent and all his belongings into a valley where they were stoned to death and then burned (Joshua 7:20-26). I am by no means suggesting we stone our brothers and sisters in Christ who disobey the Lord, but we must be aggressive with the sin that we try to hide in our own lives through genuine repentance. It is through our personal and corporate integrity that we will strengthen the Body of Christ.

Even as a surgeon will cut away some healthy tissue surrounding a cancerous growth so the disease doesn't spread, we must resolutely repent and allow the Lord to cleanse us from our rebellion. What makes us think that our compromise will go unnoticed? When we flirt with the world (wanting to clothe ourselves with "Babylonian garments" instead of the garment of praise) and take for ourselves things which the Lord says belong to Him in Haggai 2:8 ("the silver is Mine and the gold is Mine"), we bring a death sentence not only on ourselves, but also on our children and on everything we own. We must choose to live holy lives to experience God's blessings rather than curses that are self-inflicted and ushered in by unholy, fleshly desires that could contribute to our premature death.

HOW FEAR CAN BECOME
AN IDOL IN OUR LIVES

The twenty-eighth chapter of Deuteronomy clearly shows us that many of God's blessings are conditional upon whether we are faithful to <u>diligently obey</u> the voice of the Lord (verses 1-14). Conversely, if we don't obey Him, we'll bring curses upon ourselves for disobedience (verses 15-68).

Fear is not of God and originates from our fleshly, fallen nature. Tragically, this sinful nature has been passed down to all of humanity ever since Adam and Eve sinned in the Garden of Eden when they disobeyed the Lord by eating from the tree of the knowledge of good and evil (Genesis 3:1-10). Since then, every human being has had to battle fear (and every other negative coping mechanism known to man that was birthed in trepidation) in order to survive.

If we choose to not love Jesus with all of our hearts, minds, souls, and strength, then we open ourselves up to the possibility of allowing an idol to reside in our lives. How can this be, you wonder? We need to remember, first, that an idol is "a deity other than God" or "a person or thing devotedly or excessively admired." [42] Anyone or anything we worship becomes our god.

If we don't fully trust the Lord, then we simply don't trust <u>Him</u>. There is no middle ground here: either we do or we don't. If, for instance, we allow ourselves to be overwhelmed by fear repeatedly, then that's what we revere. Whomever or whatever we surrender to is whom or what we choose to glorify in our lives.

So, how does an idol make its home in a believer's life? Failure to trust Jesus just once is all that's required for the enemy to plant seeds of doubt, fear, and unbelief in our lives. I picture the enemy of our soul gloating each time we worry, grow anxious or panic about our difficult circumstances because he knows that losing our peace allows him to form a more powerful stronghold in our lives.

Often, once the trial has passed, we nonchalantly brush it off by saying, "I guess it wasn't that bad." Our enemy must chuckle when he hears this because he knows he succeeded in deceiving us through the stronghold of <u>minimizing</u>. But, if it really wasn't that bad, then why did we lose our peace to begin with? Who are we kidding? Remember, minimizing is one of many sinful defense mechanisms Satan employs in an attempt to choke out our faith.

By continuing in this deadly pattern of <u>denial</u>, we give an idol permission to grow its roots in us. What could be more frightening than to discover that besides being one with our Bridegroom, we are joined with an idol sent by Satan whose only purpose is to destroy us from within? Now that, my friends, is truly horrifying!

Have you sinned against the Lord by making a covenant with an idol as you've surrendered God's peace to fear? Have you given access to a foreign god that wants to draw you away from Jesus? Listen to the warning that the apostle Paul gives us in 1 Corinthians 10:20-22:

> …the things which the Gentiles sacrifice they
> sacrifice to demons and not to God, and I do
> not want you to have fellowship with demons.
> You cannot drink the cup of the Lord and the
> cup of demons; you cannot partake of the
> Lord's table and of the table of demons. Or
> do we provoke the Lord to jealousy? Are we
> stronger than He?

Fear usurps the role that God desires to have in our lives! The only way this evil can reside in believers' lives is if we fail to love God by not trusting Him continually to help us face our problems. How often have we felt sorry for ourselves because of the situation we're in or failed to forgive ourselves for making a wrong decision? Both of these attitudes are sinful because they doubt God's ability to fulfill His promises to us, despite our failures!

When we continue to wallow in self-pity and remain mired in the very mud from which God rescued and cleansed us from we turn our backs on the Lord by implying that His salvation and healing touch aren't good enough! When we refuse to forgive ourselves, we reject His forgiveness and deny that Jesus' sacrifice on the cross was sufficient.

We declare through our unbelieving attitude that we

don't truly believe we've been forgiven or that Jesus' blood is adequate for our cleansing, and that something more on our part must be done. Not only is this shameful, but it's prideful and rebellious, just like witchcraft! We must guard our hearts from evil influence, lest we enter into an unholy covenant with the Devil before we realize it. If we have already been purchased by Jesus' blood (1 Corinthians 6:20), there is no reason for us to go back to the same graveyard that the Lord saved us from.

These prideful mindsets actually stem from doubt and unbelief: "Will God really forgive me? If He truly knew what I was like, He wouldn't want to forgive me! Since I can't trust God, I guess I'll just have to do it myself." Ironically, we fall even deeper into fear through this negative mindset, rather than trusting the Lord to carry us through triumphantly, as did Joshua and Caleb, who were free from fear because they were solid in their faith.

TRUE SACRIFICE MEANS GIVING UP CONTROL

Far too many Christians want something—an abundant life for nothing—with no sacrifice. In short, the Church of Jesus Christ has grown spiritually lazy! We expect to see miracles but fail to pray. We desire divine wisdom but neglect reading the Holy Scriptures. We long to hear clearly from God, but wait until Sunday for Him to speak to us through a preacher rather than desperately seeking Him through fervent prayer because our very life depends on hearing from the Holy Spirit. Even worse, sometimes we don't go to church at all (because we don't feel like going) when we know we need to be strengthened spiritually by fellowshipping with other believers (Hebrews 10:25).

Such a lifestyle of self-indulgence prompts us to confess the same sins to God day after day with very little, if any, change in us and we wonder what is hindering our prayers. Part of the problem is we don't really believe God can free us from the strongholds of sin that have held us captive for years and we aren't willing to make the necessary sacrifices in our personal lives. Sometimes, watching an excessive amount of television, surfing the internet for hours, or going to too many sporting events or other social activities cuts into our prayer time with the Lord, which we need so we can be recharged spiritually the next day.

Just as feeling bad for being caught in a transgression is not the same as being remorseful for sinning, so simply confessing (admitting) our iniquity is not the same as repenting (turning from our sin where we have a change of heart so we can draw closer to God). If we're stuck confessing the same sins for years (or if we're struggling with a hurt we're too proud to admit), then perhaps we don't love God enough to make the necessary sacrifices for us to change.

Is it possible that we lust after our sin more than we love the Lord? I sincerely hope not! No coping mechanism known to man can postpone a hurt indefinitely. If covering up didn't work for Adam and Eve, why do we think it will work for us? In reality, the only thing these survival techniques do is prolong unnecessary suffering!

God hates to see us live a lie and experience needless torment that He never intended for us to suffer through. That's why the Holy Spirit continually speaks to us, warning us that these negative, self-protective behaviors are His enemies. If we refuse to listen to and obey Him, the fear of being found out will eventually eat away at our hearts and minds until it destroys us or exposes our shortcomings from the inside out.

So then, what is the cure? How do we find health and wholeness in God's kingdom? We find it through brokenness. Remember, the Lord uses the "foolish things of the world to put to shame the wise...[so] that no flesh should glory in His presence." (1 Corinthians 1:27, 29). In His kingdom, if you want to save your life, you must lose it; if you want to be the greatest, you must become as the least; if you want to receive, you must give. If you want to be whole, you must be broken! "The Lord is close to the brokenhearted and saves those who are crushed in spirit" (Psalm 34:18, New International Version).

BROKEN AND POURED OUT

A woman in the New Testament exemplifies this kind of brokenness: Mary of Bethany. John 11:2 tells us that she is the same woman who came to Jesus in Matthew 26:6, anointing His feet with oil, washing them with her tears and wiping them dry with her hair. I am extremely humbled when I think of Mary's contrite spirit. Her love for Jesus must have been deep as she wept while she washed His feet with her hair. What an amazing act of selflessness.

The Bible records that when Jesus was in Bethany that a woman approached Him with an alabaster flask of very costly fragrant oil and she poured it on His feet while He sat at a table. When He saw His disciples were indignant over the waste of such expensive oil that could have been sold to help feed the poor, the Lord quickly intervened (Matthew 26:6-9).

Jesus said to them in Matthew 26:10-13, "Why do you trouble the woman, for she has done a good work for Me. For you have the poor with you always, but Me you don't have always. For in pouring this fragrant oil on my body, she did it for My burial. Assuredly, I say to you, wherever this gospel is preached in the whole world, what this woman has done will also be told as a memorial to her."

Jesus recognized the sacrifice of Mary's heart and silenced the indignation of the others by saying that what she had done out of love for her Lord would always be remembered (Mark 14:9). Mary was preparing Jesus for the reason for which He was sent to earth by His Heavenly Father—to die for the sins of humanity. Could it be that the fragrant oil that she poured on Jesus' feet was her way of pouring out her love for her Lord? It's certainly possible.

Besides pouring out the oil on Jesus' feet, we need to remember that John 12:3 records that "…Mary took a pound of very costly oil of spikenard, anointed the feet of Jesus, and wiped His feet with her hair…" We are reminded in 1 Corinthians 11:15 that "…if a woman has long hair, it is a glory to her…for her hair is given to her for a covering."

Since Mary humbled herself to the point that she used her very own hair to wash Jesus' feet, this shows the extent to which she was willing to submit herself to the Lord, especially since her hair represented the glory of a woman. Mary offered the very best part of herself publicly. She did not hold back but gave herself completely to Jesus and her act of brokenness and humility did not go unnoticed by the Lord.

With this in mind, how many of us are willing to pour ourselves out as an offering to Jesus just like Mary did with no strings attached to honor, love and show Him that He means more to us than our families, friends, careers, goals and reputations? How many of us are willing to show Him that He means everything to us because, in reality, we have no hope or reason for living apart from God?

What a role model Mary was. Her act of love still resonates today. Can we take up the mantle this courageous woman of God left us and dare to be broken and poured out daily as a love offering for the Lord? This should be our goal because <u>Jesus desires and expects nothing less than total surrender from us.</u>

CRUSHED TO POWDER

Matthew 21:44 declares, "And whoever falls on this stone will be broken; but on whomever it falls, it will grind him to powder." I used to think this verse should be translated something like this, "You better hurry and decide to throw yourself on Jesus so there will be something remaining of you. If you don't, He'll squish you until there's nothing left!" In my ignorant thinking, grinding was a bad thing—the last alternative for the really stubborn ones!

God doesn't want to crush us but crush our pain and the things that cause our pain. He wants to fall on us when we present ourselves in complete surrender to Him so we can feel His love the way we need to be loved. The Lord wants every trace of our fears, unresolved anger and unhealthy coping behaviors to be crushed into nothingness—every hint of self-reliance, envy, hatred, and bitterness to be destroyed. Why? If we surrender completely, we'll be freer to experience His no-strings-attached, unconditional love for us and more quickly receive healing and deliverance from the pollutants of this world because we won't have any secret sins that prevent the promises of God from fully manifesting.

This reminds me of reading about a skilled potter in Bible times who was an expert at taking cracked and broken pottery that others considered worthless but to this experienced craftsman, they were valuable! He could take two or three old pots and crush them to a powder so fine that one was completely indistinguishable from the others. Then, the potter would mix the powder with oil and water to make fresh clay with which he could fashion something new and without flaw.

Author, Bryant G. Wood, PhD, writes that "As the clay yields itself to the potter, so the Christian must submit to the authority of God. When clay is first brought in from the field, it's unusable; it's hard and full of impurities. As the clay must be refined, so, too, must the Christian be refined before he can be shaped into a useful vessel by the Master Potter. Impurities have to be removed and tempering agents added; the Christian has to be softened and kneaded." [43]

In short, the Lord is the Master Potter and he shapes a believer according to His will. Since God is full of divine wisdom and knowledge, He knows how to form us in such a way that we'll be the most useful for His service.

This is how He wants to shape and perfect His Bride! After we have been crushed (died to our sinful nature), then God can add the living water or anointing oil of the Holy Spirit to form a vessel which will be strong enough to contain His power and glory without being shattered or corrupted.

In reality, we have no right to question what the Master Craftsman is doing in us because since He formed us with His own hands, He certainly knows what He's doing when He continues to shape us throughout our lives in order that we can function as an effective vessel for His glory. Isaiah 64:8 reminds us, "But now, O Lord, You are our Father; we are the clay, and You our potter; and all we are the work of Your hand."

Isaiah 57:15 declares, "For thus says the High and Lofty One Who inhabits eternity, whose name is Holy: "I dwell in the high and holy place, with him who has a contrite and humble spirit, to revive the spirit of the humble, and to revive the heart of the contrite ones" [emphasis author's]. The word in Hebrew for "contrite" is "dakka" and it literally means "crushed to powder." [44] If you've ever wondered how you could "dwell in the house of the Lord," this is the way in: You must die to yourself and be crushed to powder!

ENTERING INTO THE PROMISED LAND

Just as the Lord wanted to take the Children of Israel to their "Promised Land," He also wants to lead us out of the dry, desert places through which we've been wandering and grown comfortable with and into a place of rest in His courts. He longs to lead us into our Promised Land of great quantity and rest just as He led Joshua and Caleb to a physical place of abundance for remaining faithful to Him.

Hebrews 3:18-19, 4:1-2 begins by telling us how we fail to enter in:

> And to whom did He swear that they would not enter His rest, but to those who did not obey? So we see that they could not enter in because of unbelief. Therefore, since a promise remains of entering His rest, let us fear [be concerned] lest any of you seem to have come short of it. For indeed the gospel was preached to us as well as to them; but the word which they heard did not profit them, not being mixed with faith in those who heard it. [Emphasis author's]

Because the children of Israel refused to believe God's promise that He would be with them and deliver the nations into their hands, they could not enter their place of rest. Disobedience is the fruit of unbelief and the Israelites chose foolishly when they failed to trust the Lord for deliverance. This grave sin stems from the fear that God is unable to effectively control the circumstances or the situation.

Yes, the Israelites believed in God, but simply believing is not enough. James 2:19-20 says, "You believe that there is one God. You do well. Even the demons believe—and tremble! But do you want to know, O foolish man, that faith without works is dead?" If our belief is not translated into the action of trusting obedience, then it profits us nothing. God knows the difference between lip service and loving adoration; between pretenders and genuine contenders or servants of the Lord; between the faithless and the faithful.

Hebrews 4:9-11 declares that "There remains therefore a rest for the people of God...Let us therefore be diligent to enter that rest, lest anyone fall according to the same example of disobedience" [emphasis author's]. Mature believers are filled with God's peace and radiate the joy of the Lord because they know in their hearts that Jesus Christ loves them and they willingly humble themselves before Him. This is the key to entering the Promised Land—we prove to God that we love Him by obeying Him and living a virtuous life.

But what does that mean exactly? It means that they know their Heavenly Father loves them. It means that they dare to lay themselves upon the Lord's altar, bare every dark part of their souls before Him, and trust Him to reveal their sins and heal their deepest hurts. In essence, they allow Him to purify in a short time what they would not be able to do themselves in a lifetime because only God can forgive sins.

"FEAR NOT"

Listen to the words of encouragement that Moses gave to Joshua before all of Israel about overcoming fear as they stood on the brink of the Promised Land for the second time in Deuteronomy 31:7-8:

Be strong and of good courage, for you must go with this people to the land which the Lord has sworn to their fathers to give them, and you shall cause them to inherit it, And the Lord, He is the One who goes before you. He will be with you, He will not leave you nor forsake you; do not fear nor be dismayed. [Emphasis author's]

Notice that the one bit of advice the Lord gave to His people through Moses was "do not fear nor be dismayed." When God, Himself, spoke to Joshua after Moses died, in the space of just a few moments He said three times, "Be strong and of good courage...Only be strong and very courageous...Have I not commanded you? Be strong and of good courage" (Joshua 1:6, 7, 9)! I believe He wanted to get His point across. God was saying, "Pay attention!"

Why was the Lord so emphatic to Joshua about being courageous? It was the very sins of doubt, unbelief and fear which had kept the children of Israel from entering the land of Canaan forty years earlier and these same sins were what stood between them and their promised rest from endless wandering!

The only ones who could prevent them from obtaining the promise yet again were themselves! Remember, God never desired to see them homeless and lost in the desert and neither does He desire to see us drift aimlessly through life without any hope.

The Lord loves us today just as much as He loved that lowly group of doubting, rebellious, former slaves. Like them, God loved us when we were unlovely and He has also promised to go before us as we seek to obtain the same blessing that was promised to them. It's our rightful inheritance as His children! However, we must also keep in mind that the only ones who can keep us from entering therein and growing spiritually are ourselves.

Not even Satan has the power to prevent us from drawing closer to Jesus, even though he often tries to intimidate us into thinking that we're at his mercy. We must not forget that he is a master at deception. "There is no fear in love; but perfect love casts out fear, because fear involves torment. But he who fears has not been made perfect in love" (1 John 4:18). So, God's perfect love casts out not some, but all fear and he who fears has not yet been perfected. Since we are fearful human beings by nature, we are all a work in progress.

As the Bride of Christ, have you allowed Jesus, your Groom, to drive apprehension out of your life? There is no other way into the Promised Land of rest in Christ except through complete obedience and yielding control to Him, even when it seems foolish in the physical realm. Through total surrender, we prove our love to God.

Does that mean we'll never be afraid? Of course not! The Lord knows we're human. There's a reason why God tells us hundreds of times in the Bible to not be afraid—because He knew we would be afraid! He knows we won't win every battle with our flesh because of our fallen, sinful nature.

But He expects us to push past that fear as quickly as possible and the more battles we win against this evil influence, the more courageous and steadfast we become in our trials because of our increased trust in God. It's okay to be afraid, but it's not okay to stay afraid! The Lord understands there will be times when we give in to fear, but we can't stay there. We must slay that Goliath as soon as possible before it destroys us.

Each time we enter His throne-room through prayer, fear will become less intimidating and Jesus will become more irresistible because His love for us is like an all-consuming fire. This is how we gain strength over our weaknesses! This is how even in our brokenness we can be filled with the joy of being in God's presence; and how even in dying to our sinful nature we can be fully alive in Christ—by embracing God's love. Prayer unlocks the key in our heart that allows us to serve and worship the Lord with reckless abandon.

Joshua 24:15 declares, "choose for yourselves this day whom you will serve." We have two choices: the god of fear (Satan) or the God of Love (Jesus). You will either be found defected to the enemy's camp or perfected in Christ when you choose to trust Him with all of your worries, hurts and dreams. The Promised Land today can be found in a pure heart and it awaits you if you choose to die to your fears and dare to love the Lord with all of your heart, mind, soul and strength. The choice is yours. Will you dwell in the wilderness of fear or will you dwell in the House of the Lord? Choose the way of love, not fear, because perfect love casts out all fear!

PERFECT LOVE CASTS OUT ALL FEAR!

Take heed, My friends, and listen to the voice of the Lord,
For many have been deceived and fallen astray.
The message I now give you must not be ignored:
His grace will save you, if you choose to obey.

Have you lived your life according to the world's ways?
Have foreign voices caused you to run and hide?
Have they blinded you from the Truth and caused you to stray?
And is your way of survival really the serpent of pride?

The fruit of the Garden remains appetizing,
But the idols you've so carefully erected—
Blaming, minimizing and rationalizing—
Will leave you broken, lonely and painfully infected.

Beware of your enemies—doubt, unbelief and fear—
For, they will try to enter your heart and destroy you from
within.
Cling to faith, hope, and love when adversaries appear,
And don't be enticed by lies that tempt you to sin.

In the same way that Christ showed love and courage when He
died,
Face your hurts head-on with the innocence of a child.
Fear will flee at once when it sees God's love strings tied
To a heart that's loving, kind and undefiled.

Your obedience will part any Red Sea you must cross.
Your faith will grow as you walk forward and believe.
God is your mast, so don't worry about suffering loss;
Just trust the Holy Spirit and you won't be deceived.

David slew a mighty giant as he ran toward the Philistine.
Caleb and Joshua guaranteed victory when they were
commissioned.
As they exercised their faith God appeared on the scene;
They held on to their integrity against great opposition.

Conversely, Achan and his wife disobeyed the Word of the Lord,
Thinking they could hide their sins so no one would know.
But God saw the abominations they tried to hoard,
And for their secret sins they died as God's foes.

Die to yourself, if Heaven's your eternal goal;
Let the Lord crush you to powder through the work of His
   hands.
Allow Him to break you; give up your stubborn control
And dare to gaze into Jesus' eyes and see the Promised Land!

Hold fast in your commitment, lest you be found defected
To the enemy's camp, who desires to steal away your soul,
Love the Lord with all your heart so you can be perfected
And drink of the Living Water that'll make you whole.

Listen to the message I bring you from above:
"When you seek Me, you will find Me when you draw near.
If you love one another, I'll perfect you in My love,
And know, My child, that perfect love casts out all fear."

SPECIAL CLOSING MESSAGE

In the event that you were able to read all the way through this book and you still don't know Jesus Christ as your Lord and Savior, I would like to invite you to ask Him into your life. As you read this prayer aloud, mean it with all your heart:

Heavenly Father, I confess to You that I am a sinner in need of forgiveness for all of my sins. I'm sorry for all the ways that I have disobeyed You. I want to turn from my wicked ways and start a new life with You. I thank You that You sent Your Son, Jesus, to die on the cross in my place as the penalty for all of my sins. I accept His blood sacrifice as atonement for all the sins of my past, present, and future. I accept as truth what Jesus declared in John 14:6, "I am the way, the truth, and the life. No one comes to the Father except through Me." Therefore, I will stop striving to get to God my own way; now I choose to leave my old ways behind and I choose to walk daily in God's Way with the help of the Holy Spirit. Amen.

Congratulations! The Bible says that your name is now written in the Lamb's Book of Life and that because you have chosen to live for the Lord, you are now promised a place in Heaven! Now, you must commit yourself to live for the Lord daily with the help of the Holy Spirit.

Jesus announced in John 14:18, "I will not leave you orphans; I will come to you." The Holy Spirit now is in constant communion with your spirit (which is now alive in Christ!) to convict you whenever you sin so that you can repent immediately. He is also now always with you to comfort you during difficult times, to heal you of all kinds of pain, to guide you when you are in need of direction, and to teach you how to pray to the Father.

Now, it is time for you to start growing spiritually! Commit yourself to praying, reading and studying the Bible and establishing yourself in a sound, Christian Church where you can learn about water baptism, the baptism of the Holy Spirit, salvation, prophecy, healing and deliverance. If you are faithful to seek the will of the Lord, then out of your love for Him, the Holy Spirit will help you to live a holy life and you will experience the spiritual, emotional, physical and relational healing that you so deeply desire! I pray that God will richly bless you in your new life with Him that has just begun. God bless you!

VICTOR TORRES

ENDNOTES

CHAPTER ONE

1. *Wikipedia, the Free Encyclopedia, Death Wish* (Film Series), Wikimedia Foundation, Inc., December 24, 2013, p. 1.

2. The Journal Sentinel, Flip Wilson: "What You Saw Wasn't All You Got," Chris Foran, Milwaukee, Georgia: JSOnline. com, April 17, 2013, p. 1

3. *Wikipedia, the Free Encyclopedia*, Matthew 3:12, Wikimedia Foundation, Inc.

4. *Random House Webster's College Dictionary*, New York: Random House, Inc., 1999. p. 6.

5. Viacom Entertainment Group, *About All in the Family*, Canada, Viacom International Inc., TV Land.com, 2014, p. 1.

6. Ibid.

CHAPTER TWO

7. Ruth Ward Heflin, *Glory, Experiencing the Atmosphere of Heaven*, Hagerstown, Maryland: McDougal Press, 1997, pp. 87-88.

8. Daniel B. Wallace, *Bible.org*, "What Does It Mean to Be Justified? A Brief Exposition of Romans 3:21-26, Part 2," Richardson, Texas: Biblical Studies Foundation, July 17th, 2007.

9. Larry Crabb, *Inside Out*, Colorado Springs, Colorado: NAV Press, 1988, pp. 66.

CHAPTER THREE

10. Dick Eastman, *No Easy Road*, Grand Rapids, Michigan: Baker Book House, 1987, p. 32

11. Ibid.

12. Walt Kelly, "We Have Met the Enemy and He Is Us," *Post Hall Syndicate*, 1970.

13. Mel Brooks, *History of the World Part I*, Brooksfilms, 20th Century Fox, Los Angeles, California, 1981.

14. Glenn T. Stanton, *Crosswalk.com*, "The Christian Divorce Rate Myth," Salem, Oregon, Stanton Baptist Press, March 20, 2012.

15. Bradley R.E. Wright, *Christians Are Hate-Filled Hypocrites...and Other Lies You've Been Told: a Sociologist Shatters Myths From the Secular and Christian Media*, Minneapolis, MN: Bethany House, 2010, p. 133.

16. Paul Goulet, *Reconciling Man To God—Reconcilers Training Series Manual I*, Reconcilers Training Ministries, Inc., 1991, p. 53.

17. Ibid.

18. Walt Disney, *Bambi*, Walt Disney Studio Inc., Burbank, California, 1942.

CHAPTER FOUR

19. Graham Cooke, Sunday morning sermon at Family Christian Center, Orangevale, CA, November 8, 1998.

20. Ibid.

21. Ibid.

22. Ibid.

23. Ibid.

24. Ibid.

25. Edwin Louis Cole, *Maximized Manhood: A Guide to Family Survival*, Dallas Texas, 1988, audio tape #3.

26. David Wilkerson, Delivered From This Present Evil World!, Times Square Pulpit Series, March 25, 1996.

27. Graham Cooke, Sunday morning sermon at Family Christian Center, Orangevale, CA, November 8, 1998.

CHAPTER FIVE

28. Smith Wigglesworth, *Ever Increasing Faith*, Springfield, Missouri, 1971, p. 43.

29. Henry Halley, *Halley's Bible Handbook*, Grand Rapids, Michigan: Zondervan Publishing House, 1984, p. 607.

30. *The Bantam Medical Dictionary*, New York: Bantam Books, 1994, p. 303.

31. Kenneth Haggin, "A teaching on healing at Calvary Christian Center," Sacramento, CA, August 18, 1997.

32. David Wilkerson, *Delivered From This Present Evil World*, Times Square Pulpit Series, March 25, 1996.

33. Graham Cooke, Sunday morning sermon at Family Christian Center, Orangevale, CA, November 8, 1998.

34. *Strong's Exhaustive Concordance of the Bible*, Hebrew and Chaldee Dictionary, Riverside Book and Bible House, 1980, p. 50.

35. Ibid., p. 86-87.

CHAPTER SIX

36. Edwin Louis Cole, *Maximized Manhood: A Guide to Family Survival*, Dallas, Texas, 1988, audio tape #3.

37. Ibid.

38. Ibid.

39. Phillip Keller, *A Shepherd Looks At Psalm 23*, Grand Rapids, Michigan: Zondervan Publishing House, 1970, pp. 32-33.

40. Ibid., p. 33.

41. Ibid., p. 34.

42. *Random House College Dictionary*, 1999, p.654.

43. Bryant G. Wood, PhD, The Master Potter: Pottery Making in the Bible, *Bible Archaelogy.org*, July 05, 2011, pp. 6-7.

44. Friedrich Wilhem Gesenuis, *Hebrew and Chaldee Dictionary*. Word number 1793, p. 30.

SOURCES

Burgoon, Judee K. & Thomas Saine. *The Unspoken Dialogue: An Introduction to Non-Verbal Communication.* University of Florida: Houghton Mifflin Company, 1978.

Chapman, Gary, *The 5 Love Languages: The Secret to Love That Lasts*, Chicago, Illinois: Northfield Publishing, 2010.

Cole, Edwin Lewis. *Maximized Manhood: A Guide to Family Survival*, audio cassette series. Dallas, Texas, 1988.

Colson, Chuck. *Jubilee*. Washington, D.C.: Prison Fellowship Ministries, November 1996.

Crabb, Larry. *Inside Out.* Colorado Springs, Colorado: NAV Press, 1988.

Crabtree, Charles. "The Value of A Human Soul." Sermon at Harvest Church, Elk Grove, CA. December 1, 1996.

Eastman, Dick. *No Easy Road.* Grand Rapids, Michigan: Baker Book House, 1987.

Eggerichs, Emerson, *Love & Respect*, Nashville, Tennessee, Thomas Nelson, 2004.

Foxe, John. *Foxe's Book of Martyrs.* Old Tappan, New Jersey: Fleming H. Revell Company, 1976.

Goulet, Paul. *Reconciling Man to God—Reconcilers Training Series*, Manual I. Sacramento: Reconcilers Training Ministries, Inc, 1996.

Goulet, Paul. *Reconciling Man to Others—Reconcilers Training Series*, Manual III. Sacramento: Reconcilers Training Ministries, Inc, 1988.

Grinder, Michael & Associates. "Presentation Skills Workshop." National Training Association of Sebastapol, California.

June 1995.

Hagan, Scott. An Address to the Congregation. Harvest Church, Elk Grove, CA. December 1, 1996.

Hagin, Kenneth. A Teaching on Healing. Calvary Christian Center, Sacramento, CA. August 18, 1997.

Halley, Henry. *Halley's Bible Handbook*. Grand Rapids, Michigan: Zondervan Publishing House, 1984.

Heflin, Ruth Ward. *Glory, Experiencing the Atmosphere of Heaven*. Hagerstown, Maryland: McDougal Publishing Company, 1997.

Holy Bible, New International Version. Grand Rapids, Michigan: Zondervan Publishing House, 1984.

Holy Bible, New King James Version. Nashville, Tenn.: Thomas Nelson Publishers, 1983.

Keller, Phillip. *A Shepherd Looks At Psalm 23*. Grand Rapids, Michigan: Zondervan Publishing House, 1970.

Law Terry. *The Power of Praise and Worship*. Tulsa, Oklahoma: Victory House, Inc, 1985.

Stanley, Andy, *The New Rules For Love, Sex & Dating CD*, Alpharetta, Georgia: North Point Ministries, Inc., 2011.

Random House Webster's College Dictionary. New York: Random House, Inc, 1999.

Rosenthal, Robert, Hall, Judith A.DiMatteo, M. Robin, Rogers, Peter L. *Sensitivity to Nonverbal Communication: The Pons Test*. Baltimore & London: The John Hopkins University Press, 1979.

Sadalla, Gail, Meg Holmburg, and Jim Halligan. "How to Construct an I-Message." *Conflict Resolution: An Elementary School Curriculum*. The Community Board

Program, Inc, 1990.

Strong, James. *The Exhaustive Concordance of The Bible*. Iowa Falls, Iowa: Word Bible Publishers.

The Bantam Medical Dictionary. New York: Bantam Books, 1994.

The One Year Bible, New International Version. Wheaton, Illinois: Tyndale House Publishers, Inc, 1984.

Torres, Victor. *A Comparative Analysis Between Born-Again, Spirit-Filled Christian and Secular Humanistic Counseling*. Master's Thesis. California State University, Sacramento, Sacramento, California, 1987.

Wigglesworth, Smith. *Ever Increasing Faith*. Springfield, Missouri: The Gospel Publishing House, 1971.

Wilkerson, David. Times Square Pulpit Series Newsletters. Lindale, Texas: World Challenge Ministries, June 26, 1995 & March 25, 1996.

ABOUT THE AUTHOR, VICTOR TORRES

Victor Torres is a professional counselor with twenty-four years of experience. He graduated from California State University, Sacramento with a double Master's Degree in Marriage, Family, and Child Counseling and School Counseling in May 1987 and a double Bachelor's Degree in Social Work and Spanish in January 1981. He also earned three Community College Credentials in Counseling, Counseling Supervising and Psychology through the Los Rios Community College District in 1987.

During these years as a helping professional, he has received thirteen national awards for dedication, performance, leadership and distinguished service as an exceptional counselor, author, and public speaker from Covington Who's Who Executive of the Year (2014) Covington Who's Who Professional and Executive of the Year (2013), Covington Who's Who (2013, 2012), Worldwide Who's Who (2013) Strathmore's Who's Who (2012, 2000-2001), Who's Who Among America's Teachers (2004-2005, 1996), Metropolitan's Who's Who (2006), Who's Who Among Human Service Professionals (1992, 1988) and The National Distinguished Service Registry (1990). He is also a published Lifetime Member of the International Society of Poets (1996).

Victor is a Spirit-filled Christian who has experienced the Lord's powerful touch in his life in the areas of emotional and physical healing. "In the last twenty-four years, as I have counseled people of all ages and at nearly every stage of life, I have found one common theme to all the various hurts reported to me by my clients: because they have been hurt by others, they allow fear to rule their hearts. Then, defeat and despair settle in, and they remain in the bondage of merely existing, rather than allowing the Great Physician to heal them, free them, and give them an abundant life in Christ."

Victor believes that this book will radically change lives by leading many to freedom from fear into a vibrant relationship with Jesus Christ that embraces openness, honesty, integrity, and Christ's perfect love fully manifest. He also believes that this manuscript will be used greatly by the Lord to usher in spiritual revival for those who are hungry for God and desire to see the Holy Spirit manifest Himself mightily through miraculous healings, deliverance, salvation, and prophecy.

He currently lives in Elk Grove, California with his three children, Joshua, Rachel and Jonathan.

To contact Victor to either purchase his materials or to have him come speak, visit him at Armed4Battle.com, Perfectlovecastsoutallfear.com or at Amazon.com. He would love to hear from you!

AUTHOR, PUBLIC SPEAKER,
& COUNSELOR
VICTOR TORRES

66217536R00099

Made in the USA
Lexington, KY
07 August 2017